JOHN HENRY NEWMAN

Newman reading J. R. Seeley's *Ecce Homo*, 1866

JOHN HENRY NEWMAN

A very brief history

EAMON DUFFY

First published in Great Britain in 2019

Society for Promoting Christian Knowledge
36 Causton Street
London SW1P 4ST
www.spck.org.uk

British Library Cataloguing-in-Publication Data
A catalogue record for this book is available from the British Library

ISBN 978 0 281 07849 3
eBook ISBN 978 0 281 07850 9

1 3 5 7 9 10 8 6 4 2

Typeset by The Book Guild Ltd, Leicester
Printed in Great Britain by TJ International, Padstow, Cornwall

eBook by The Book Guild Ltd, Leicester

Produced on paper from sustainable forests

In piam memoriam

Hamish F. G. Swanston and
Charles Stephen Dessain, Cong. Orat.
who led me to Newman

Contents

Chronology

1801	February 21, born at Old Broad Street, London, eldest of six children of John Newman (*d.* 1824), banker, and of Jemima (*d.* 1836), daughter of Henry Fourdrinier, paper maker.
1808	(Until 1816), at Ealing School, a private boarding school.
1816	March. Financial collapse of his father's bank.
	Early August to December 21, serious illness. Evangelical conversion under the influence of classics master, the Rev Walter Meyers.
1817	(Until 1820), enters Trinity College, Oxford.
1818	May. College scholarship
	November 4, publishes with J. W. Bowden *St Bartholomew's Eve*, an anti-Catholic narrative poem.
1820	November, breakdown during Schools (finals), gains a fourth in Classics.
1822	April 12, elected to a Fellowship by examination at Oriel College.
1823	April, E. B. Pusey elected Fellow of Oriel.
1824	June 23, Trinity Sunday, Newman ordained deacon, becomes curate of St Clements parish in east Oxford.
	September 29, death of John Newman senior.
1825	March, Vice-Principal, St Alban Hall, under

Richard Whately.

1824–6 Articles for *Encyclopaedia Metropolitana* on Cicero, Apolonius of Tyana, and miracles in the Bible.

1825 Whit Sunday, ordained priest of Church of England.

1826 Publication of Whately's *Elements of Logic* (1826), with assistance from Newman. Newman appointed Tutor of Oriel. Hurrell Froude elected Fellow of Oriel.

1826 July 2, first university sermon, 'The Philosophical Temper first enjoined by the Gospel'.

1827 Publication of John Keble's *The Christian Year*. November, breakdown from overwork.

1828 January 5, death of Newman's sister Mary.
February, Edward Hawkins elected Provost of Oriel.
March 14, Newman becomes Vicar of University Church (St Mary the Virgin).
Summer, Newman begins systematic reading of the Fathers.

1829 January, 'Poetry, with reference to Aristotle's Poetics', in *London Review*.
February, Newman joins successful campaign to oust Sir Robert Peel as MP for Oxford, because of his support for Catholic Emancipation.
March, Catholic Emancipation Act: Newman elected Secretary of Oxford branch of the evangelical Church Missionary Society.

1830 February 1, publishes *Suggestions on Behalf of the Church Missionary Society*.
March 8, deposed as Secretary of Oxford branch

of CMS.

June, Newman resigns membership of Bible Society: Provost Hawkins suspends supply of pupils to Newman.

1831 Commissioned by Hugh James Rose to write a History of the General Councils.

1832 December 8, commences Mediterranean tour with Archdeacon and Hurrell Froude.

1833 March, visits Nicholas Wiseman at Venerable English College in Rome.

April, Sicily, Newman contracts typhoid.

June, composes 'Lead Kindly Light' aboard ship for England.

Reform Act passed in England.

July 9, return to England.

July 14, Keble's Assize Sermon 'On National Apostacy'.

July 25–28, Hadleigh Conference, key moment in the emergence of the 'Oxford Movement'.

August, publishes first essay of *The Church of the Fathers* in the *British Magazine*.

September 9, Newman publishes the first three *Tracts for the Times*.

October 29, Tracts 6 and 7 'The Episcopal Church Apostolical'.

November 4 and 11, Tracts 10 and 11.

November 5, Publication of *Arians of the Fourth Century*: Hurrell Froude departs for West Indies.

December 13 and 23, Tracts 15 and 19, *Apostolical Succession*.

December 24, Tract 20, *The Visible Church*.

1834 January 1, Tract 21, *Mortification of the Flesh a*

duty.

Lyra Apostolica – volume of verses with Keble and others.

March, publishes first volume of *Parochial Sermons.*

April 25, Tract 31, *The Reformed Church.*

May 1, Tracts 33 and 34, *Primitive Epsicopacy, Rites and Customs.*

June, Newman refuses to solemnize marriage of Miss Jubber, as an unbaptized person.

June 25, August 24, Tracts 38 and 41, *The Via Media.*

September, Newman begins published correspondence with the Abbe Jaeger.

November 1, Tract 47, *Visible Church.*

1835 March, publishes *The Restoration of Suffragan Bishops Recommended* and second volume of *Parochial Sermons.*

May, defeat of proposal to admit Dissenters to Oxford University.

1836 January, Volume 3 of *Parochial Sermons*, Tract 71, *Controversy with Romanists.*

February 2, Tract 73, *Introduction of Rationalist Principles into Religion.*

February 13, publishes (anonymously) *Elucidations of Dr Hamden's Theological Statements.*

February 17, Hamden appointed Regius Professor of Divinity at Oxford.

February 28, death of Hurrell Froude.

April, *British Critic* review, Le Bas *Life of Laud.*

April 25, Tract 74, *Catena Patrum on Apostolic Succession.*

Summer, Newman commences *Lectures on Prophetical Office of the Church* in Adam de Brome chapel.
June 24, Tract 75, on the Roman Breviary.
July, *British Critic* 'Brothers Controversy' on Apostolic Tradition.
Reviews in *British Critic* Burton's *History of the Christian Church.*
October, *British Critic* review of Wiseman's *Lectures on the Catholic Church.*

1837 March, *Lectures on Prophetical Office* published.
March 25, Tract 79, On Purgatory.
June 25, publishes Letter to Dr Geoffrey Faussett.
July, *British Critic* review of *Life of Franke.*
October, *British Critic* review, de Lamennais, *Affairs of Rome.*
November 1, Tract 82, defence of Pusey on Baptism.

1838 January, Newman takes over as editor of *British Critic.*
February, Vols 1 and 2 of Froude's *Remains* published (Newman and Keble, eds).
March 30, *Lectures on Justification* published.
June 29, Tract 83, Advent sermons on AntiChrist.
July, *British Critic* review of *Geraldine, a tale of Conscience.*
British Critic review of Ingram's *Memorials of Oxford.*
British Critic review of *Random Recollections of Exeter Hall.*
August, Bishop Bagot of Oxford's *Charge* on the Tracts.
September, consecration of Newman's new chapel

at Littlemore.
September 21, Tract 85, *Scripture Proof of the Doctrines of the Church.*
October, *British Critic* review of Palmer's *Treatise on the Church of Christ.*
November, Golightly begins subscription for the Oxford Martyr's Memorial.
Volume 4, *Parochial Sermons.*

1839 Newman edits *Catechetical Lectures of St Cyril* (translated by R. W. Church) and *Treatises of St Cyprian*, for the Library of the Fathers.
January, Newman collects and re-publishes his anti-Roman utterances.
British Critic review of Jacobson's *Apostolical Fathers – Ignatius.*
April, Newman publishes 'State of Religious Parties', *British Critic.*
British Critic review of Elliott's *Travels in Three Great Empires.*
August, Wiseman's *Dublin Review* article on 'The Anglican Claim to Apostolical Succession'.
October, *British Critic* article, 'The Anglo-American Church'.
Review of *Brief Memoir of Nicholas Ferrar.*

1840 January, *British Critic* article, 'Catholicity of the English Church', a reply to Wiseman.
March 25, Tract 88, *Bishop Andrewes' Devotions.*
May, acquires 9 acres of land at Littlemore and converts a row of cottages into an informal 'monastery'.
July, *British Critic* review of books on 'Persecution of Protestants in Germany'.

October, Volume 5, *Parochial Sermons.*
British Critic review of *Life of Countess of Huntingdon.*
British Critic review of Todd's *Discourses on Antichrist.*

1841 January, *British Critic* review of Milman's *History of Christianity.*
January 25, Tract 90, on subscription to the 39 Articles.
February, Letters to the Times by 'Catholicus' *On the Tamworth Reading Room.*
March 13, Newman's Letter to R. W. Jelf on Tract 90.
March 16, university authorities condemn Tract 90.
March 29, letter to the Bishop of Oxford on Tract 90.
April, *British Critic* review of Bowden's *Gregory VII.*
July, Episcopal condemnations of Tract 90 begin.
British Critic article, 'Private Judgement'.
British Critic review of Aquinas's *Catena Aurea.*
October 5, Jerusalem Bishopric authorized by Parliament.

1842 Newman translates *Select Treatises of S. Athanasius vol 1*, for the Library of the Fathers.
February, Newman moves to Littlemore. Publishes volume 6, *Parochial Sermons*: translation of Fleury's *Ecclesiastical History* with prefatory *Essay on Ecclesiastical Miracles* (reissued in separate format 1843).
April, *British Critic* review *Works of John Davison.*

1843 Newman translates *S. Athanasius Historical*

Treatises for the Library of the Fathers.
January, prints unsigned retraction of his anti-Roman writings in *The Conservative Journal*.
February 2, preaches university sermon on 'The Theory of Developments in Religious Doctrine'.
Late February, publishes *Oxford University Sermons*.
May, informs Keble that he believed Roman Catholic Church 'the Church of the Apostles'.
September 18, resigns St Mary's, preaches at Littlemore September 25, his last Anglican sermon, 'The Parting of Friends': publishes prospectus to *The Lives of the British Saints*.
Late 1843, *Sermons on Subjects of the Day*.

1844 Newman translates *Select Treatises of S. Athanasius vol 2. Library of the Fathers*.
February, Convocation of University condemns Ward's *Ideal* and strips him of his degrees. Censure of Tract 90 vetoed by Proctors.

1845 June, W. G. Ward publishes *Ideal of a Christian Church*.
September, death of John Bowden, Newman's oldest Oxford friend.
October 3, resigns Fellowship at Oriel.
October 9, received into the Catholic Church by Fr Dominic Barberi.
November 1, Newman confirmed by Wiseman at Oscott.
November, *Essay on Development* published.

1846 February 22, leaves Littlemore, moves to Old Oscott (Maryvale) near Birmingham.
September, leaves England for Rome.
November enrolls at College of *Propaganda Fide*

to prepare for ordination.

1847 May 30, ordained RC priest.

October 10, appointed Superior of the English Oratory of St Philip.

December 24, arrives in London.

1848 February 1, Oratory established at Maryvale. Frederick Faber and companions admitted 14 February.

February 21, Publishes *Loss and Gain, the Story of a Convert*.

1849 January 26, moves the Oratory to former gin distillery, Alcester St., Birmingham. London Oratory settles in King William Street under Frederick Faber.

1850 March 9, Gorham Judgement in Court of Arches.

May 9, begins the polemical lectures *On Certain Difficulties felt by Anglicans in submitting to the Catholic Church* at the London Oratory.

September 29, Restoration of the Catholic Hierarchy in England.

1851 April, H. E. Manning becomes a Catholic.

June 30, Newman begins *Lectures on the Present Position of Catholics in England* in the Birmingham Corn Exchange.

July 18, Newman invited by Archbishop Cullen to become Rector of Catholic University in Dublin.

August, Evangelical Alliance initiates prosecution of Newman for libel against apostate Dominican Giovanni Achilli.

November 12, Newman appointed Rector of the Catholic University of Ireland.

1852 February, Oratory moves to Hagley Road,

Edgbaston.
May 10, begins lectures on *The Idea of a University* at the Dublin Rotunda.
June 24, the Achilli Trial, Newman found guilty of libel.
July 13, Newman delvers his sermon on 'The Second Spring' at the first Synod of the restored Catholic hierarchy at Oscott.

1853 February 2, *Discourse on the Scope and Nature University Education* published, 'one of my two most perfect works, artistically' [the other was *Lectures on the Present Position of Catholics*, his most amusing book].
October-November, Liverpool lectures *On the History of the Turks in its Relation to Christianity* (pub. 1854).

1854 March, Newman's letters to *Catholic Standard* 'Who's to Blame', on the Crimean conflict.
Begins *Catholic University Gazette.*

1855 October, quarrel between London and Birmingham Oratories begins, formal separation 1856.

1856 Early 1856, *Callista, a Tale of the Third Century* (published anonymously).
June 29, opening of Newman's University Church in Dublin.

1857 Publishes *Sermons preached on Various Occasions.*
August, commissioned by Wiseman and bishops to oversee Catholic translation of the bible.

1858 January 1, Launches university periodical, *The Atlantis*. Article on 'The Mission of St Benedict'.
January-March, publishes six leading articles on 'The Catholic University' in H. Wilberforce's

Weekly Register.
July, declines to attend Aldenham meeting with the liberal Catholics Acton and Dollinger.
Publishes 'St Cyril's Formula' in *Atlantis*.
November 12, resigns as rector of the Catholic University.

1859 March, accepts editorship of *The Rambler*.
July, publishes article 'On Consulting the Laity in Matters of Doctrine'. Resigns editorship. Delated to Rome for heresy by Bishop Brown of Newport.
Opens Oratory School, Edgbaston.

1860 May, Bishop Ullathorne proposes establishment of a Catholic mission in Oxford.
Autumn, Benjamin Jowett publishes *Essays and Reviews* by seven Anglican Liberals.

1862 June, publishes disclaimer in *The Globe* newspaper of any intention of leaving the Oratory to return to the Church of England.

1863 August, Malines Congress (Liberal Catholic conference, key speeches by Montalambert, Dollinger).
September 26, death of Fr Faber.
December, Kingsley attacks Newman in *Macmillan's Magazine*.

1864 February 12, Newman publishes his correspondence with Kingsley as pamphlet.
March 5, 'Munich Brief' of Pio Nono (Pope Pius IX), attacking Liberal Catholicism.
March 20, Kingsley publishes *What, then, does Dr Newman mean?*
March 31, Newman begins writing the *Apologia*.
April 21, first part of *Apologia* published as

pamphlet.
June 16, eighth and final weekly part of *Apologia* published.
October, Newman buys land in Oxford for a College and church.
December 8, promulgation of encyclical *Quanta cura* by Pius IX, with the *Syllabus of Errors*.

1865 February 15, death of Cardinal Wiseman.
May 8, Henry Edward Manning appointed Archbishop of Westminster.
May, first part of *Dream of Gerontius* appears in *The Month*.
September, Pusey's *Eirenicon*.

1866 January, Newman publishes *Letter to Dr Pusey* (on Catholic devotion to the Virgin).
October, Newman preaches 'The Pope and the Revolution' on the Temporal Power.

1867 June 26, Pope Pius IX announces calling of 1st Vatican Council.
August, Propaganda Fide declares English Catholic attendance at Oxford 'a proximate occasion of mortal sin'.

1868 January, *Verses on Various Occasions*.
October, Newman declines invitation to attend Council as Consultor.
W. J. Copeland (Newman's former curate) begins republication of *Parochial and Plain Sermons* (8 vols.).

1869 Copeland reissues *Sermons Bearing on Subjects of the Day*.

1870 January 28, private letter to Ullathorne against the definition of Infallibility.

	March 15, publication of *Grammar of Assent*.
	July 18, promulgation of Papal Infallibility.
	September 20, surrender of Papal Rome to Kingdom of Italy.
1872	*Discussions and Arguments on Various Subjects*
	New and expanded edition of *Fifteen Sermons Preached before the University of Oxford*.
1874	November 5, Gladstone, *Vatican Decrees in their Bearing on Civil Allegiance*.
	January 14, Newman's *Letter to the Duke of Norfolk*.
1875	May 24, death of Ambrose St John.
1877	August, *Preface to the Third Edition of the Via Media*.
	December 15, elected first Honorary Fellow of Trinity College Oxford.
1878	February 7, death of Pio Nono.
	February 20, Giachino Pecchi elected Pope Leo XIII.
1879	March 15, Newman formally offered Cardinalate, and accepts.
	May 12, Newman's red hat confirmed, as Cardinal Deacon of S. Georgio in Vellabro, in Consistory in Rome: he makes the Biglietto speech on his lifelong battle against 'liberalism'.
1882	June, Tom Mozley's *Reminiscences Chiefly of Oriel College and the Oxford Movement*.
1884	February, 'On the Inspiration of Scripture', in *The Nineteenth Century*.
1885	May, A. M. Fairbairn attacks Newman's 'philosophical skepticism' in *The Contemporary Review*.
	October, Newman replies with 'Revelation in its

relation to Faith'.

1890 August 11, 8.45p.m., Newman dies of pneumonia. August 19, buried at Rednall in the grave of Ambrose St John.

1

Introduction

A prophet to two Churches

John Henry Newman's intellectual journey was one of the most remarkable of the nineteenth century. As Vicar of the University Church in Oxford and a university teacher, between 1833 and 1843 he was the key theorist and the most vigorous propagandist of 'Tractarianism', the Oxford-based movement to re-Catholicize the Protestant Church of England. This 'Oxford Movement' would transform Anglicanism in Newman's own lifetime. His influence within the Roman Catholic Church, which he entered in October 1845, took much longer to make its impact. He was, by nineteenth century Catholic standards, a deeply unconventional thinker. His first intellectual influences had come from the radical figures of the English and Scottish enlightenment – Hume, Gibbon, Thomas Paine. They in turn gave way to the powerful religious impact of Anglican Evangelicalism, and he acknowledged a life-long debt to Evangelical classics like the *Church History* of Joseph and Isaac Milner,[1] and the conversion narrative and biblical commentaries of Thomas Scott. But though he was convinced that his own teenage evangelical conversion in 1816 was the beginning of his serious religious life, Newman outgrew both his childish drift towards unbelief and his adolescent evangelicalism. From 1828 onwards he immersed himself in the writings of the Greek Fathers, and reacted against both the anti-dogmatic liberalism and the emotional subjectivity which he saw as the twin evils of modern Protestantism. In due course, after his conversion to Catholicism, he would be equally resistant to the scholastic mindset and insistence on a centralized papal autocracy which between them cramped the Catholicism of his day.

Newman was one of the first Christian theologians to grasp the historical contingency of all theological formulations, even the Creeds, which he characterized as 'the truth as far as they go, and under the conditions of thought which human feebleness imposes'. So as a Catholic, he rejected doctrinaire demands for unquestioning obedience to contemporary church formulae as if they were timeless truths. In an authoritarian church he was an ardent defender of the legitimate autonomy of the theologian, and, in a clericalist age, insisted on the role of the laity as custodians and not mere recipients of the faith of the Church. He was scathingly and increasingly critical of the ethos of the Church under Pope Pius IX, and he opposed the definition of Papal Infallibility in 1870, as an unnecessary and inappropriate burden on consciences. 'We have come to a climax of tyranny', he wrote, 'It is not good for a Pope to live 20 years… he becomes a God and has no-one to contradict him.'[2] The appetite of the pro-papal 'Ultramontane' party for new dogmatic definitions seemed to Newman the sign of a lack of intellectual integrity, 'the act of a man who will believe anything because he believes nothing, and is ready to profess whatever his ecclesiastical, that is his political, party requires of him…'[3]

The First Vatican Council was the climax of much that Newman deplored in the Catholicism of his day. By contrast, it has become a theological truism that the Second Vatican Council, with its reforming impulses, its outreach to other churches and faith traditions, its emphasis on the role of the laity, and its move away from papal and clerical authoritarianism, was 'Newman's Council', the moment when many of the ideas which he first championed became the basis for a radical re-imagining of what it was to be Catholic. Although he was surprisingly seldom quoted in the Conciliar debates at Vatican II, his ideas had undoubtedly been absorbed by some of its key protagonists, and the Council endorsed his central theological idea, the development of doctrine.

Born in 1801, and living till 1890, Newman's career spanned almost the whole nineteenth century, and what were then two different worlds, Protestant and Catholic. In both, he was a force for unsettlement. We think of him as a Victorian, but, like his younger contemporary Dickens, he was in fact a product of Regency England: he was 36 years old when the teenage Victoria came to the throne, and by then already a famous man. He could remember candles placed in windows to celebrate Nelson's victory at the Battle of Trafalgar in 1805, he read the novels of Austen and Scott and the poems of Byron as they first appeared, he was twenty years old when Schleiermacher published his magnum opus *The Christian Faith* (though Newman almost certainly never read a word of it) and he had reached the pinnacle of his pre-eminence within the Church of England before the young Victoria's accession in 1837. A remarkably consistent thinker, to the end of his life Newman looked back on his evangelical conversion in 1816 as the saving of his soul. Yet as a Fellow of Oriel, the most intellectually prestigious of the Oxford Colleges which he joined in 1822, he rejected Calvinism and came to see Evangelicalism, with its emphasis on religious feeling and on the reformation doctrine of Justification by Faith alone, as opening the way to an undogmatic religious individualism which ignored the Church's role in the transmission of revealed truth, and which he believed must lead inexorably to subjectivism and unbelief. Much of his writing as an Anglican was directed at undermining what he came to see as the undue influence of the 'Peculiars', as he dubbed evangelicals, within the Church of England.

Yet despite his suspicion of Evangelical emphasis on the religion of the heart as opposed to the head, Newman himself was a child of the Romantic era. Notoriously, he believed that his evangelical conversion had had a life-long effect on him, in 'making me rest in the thought of two and two only supreme and luminously self-evident beings, myself and my Creator.' As a Cardinal he chose as the motto on his coat of arms a phrase from St Francois de Sales – *Cor ad cor loquitur* (Heart speaks to heart). In his early twenties, partly as an antidote to his own instinctively sceptical cast of mind, he sought objective religious truth initially in a romanticized version of the Anglican High Church tradition, emphasising the mystery of God, the beauty and necessity of personal holiness, and the centrality of the Church's sacraments and teaching for salvation. Eloquent, learned, widely read, combining a beautiful voice with an unmatched mastery of words, by the early 1830s Newman's preaching had acquired a cult following in Oxford. *Credo in Newmanum* became an undergraduate slogan, and admiring undergraduates imitated even his eccentricities, like his habit of kneeling down abruptly as if his knees had given way. The University authorities became alarmed, and changed College timetables so that undergraduates had to choose between hearing Newman preach and eating their dinners. In their hundreds, they chose the preaching. This was all the more remarkable since Newman's message was both uncompromisingly austere, and often deliberately provocative, as in his 1832 Sermon on *The Religion of the Day*:

> Here I will not shrink from uttering my firm conviction, that it would be a gain to this country, were it vastly more superstitious, more bigoted, more gloomy, more fierce in its religion, than at present it shows itself to be. Not, of course, that I think the tempers of mind herein implied desirable, which would be an evident absurdity; but I think them infinitely more desirable and more promising than a heathen obduracy, and a cold, self-sufficient, self-wise tranquillity ... The fear of God is the beginning of wisdom; till you see Him to be a consuming fire, and approach Him with reverence and godly fear, as being sinners, you are not even in sight of the strait gate. I do not wish you to be able to point to any particular time when you renounced the world (as it is called), and were converted; this is a deceit. Fear and love must go together; always fear, always love, to your dying day.[4]

It could be argued quite plausibly that his Anglican sermons were Newman's greatest achievement. Professor Owen Chadwick called the parochial and plain sermons 'the most important publication not only of Newman's Protestant days but of his life' and thought that taken as a body of reflection on the Christian life and the quest for "reality in religion", the sermons stood comparison with the greatest devotional classics in the language.[5] Preached over a period of fifteen years, they trace Newman's own religious development as he moved decisively away from his early Evangelicalism, under the influence in particular of the Alexandrian

Fathers, whom he was studying intensively in Greek in these years. The Christology and ecclesiology of the sermons was heavily indebted to Greek thought, and in particular the Alexandrian insistence, exotic to the nineteenth century English religious imagination, that human nature had been divinized by Christ's incarnation, redemptive death and resurrection.

Yet alongside this theologically rich and often sublime preaching, Newman was also a ferocious, and sometimes unscrupulous pamphleteer and polemicist. The role of provocateur came naturally to him, and he quickly established himself as the fieriest spirit of a determined group of like-minded High-Church clergy in Oxford, which included his Oriel colleague John Keble, Oxford Professor of Poetry from 1831–1841 and the Regius Professor of Hebrew, Edward Bouverie Pusey. Disgusted by the weakening of the National Church by political concessions to Dissenters and Roman Catholics, they claimed the religious loyalty of the nation, not as earlier high-churchmen had done, on the basis of the Church of England's legal Establishment, but on a new awareness of the Church's 'Apostolical descent'.

Newman's sacramentalism was deepened by the sanctified Wordsworthian romanticism of Keble's *Christian Year*, organized round the calendar and contents of the Book of Common Prayer, and Victorian England's best-selling book of verse. He was egged on in a more radically populist direction by another Oriel colleague, Richard Hurrell Froude, son of a west-country archdeacon, and a flamboyant agitator who practised extreme asceticism, prayed the Roman Breviary in Latin every day, despised the Protestant reformers, denounced the Church of England's reformation as 'a limb badly set' which 'must be broken again before it can be righted', and ridiculed the staid establishmentarianism of the older 'High and Dry' churchmen, whom he labelled 'the Zs'. Newman revered Pusey's learning and Keble's sanctity: but he loved and idolized Froude, after whose death from TB in 1836, aged only 33, Newman would never again have a friend or colleague to whom he would look for leadership: from now on, he would suffer that worst of isolations, to have no equals, only disciples. But in 1833 Froude was at his most ebullient, and under his influence Newman and his associates stole a populist device from their evangelical opponents. They launched a series of short polemical 'Tracts for the Times', designed to re-educate clergy and laity about the value of Catholic doctrines, sacraments and rituals which, till then, most Protestants had associated with superstition and popery. Newman soon came to reject the label 'Protestant' for the C of E, and that rejection was to increase suspicion that he and his friends were fifth columnists for popery within the established church.

A single-minded campaigner, Newman was far from fastidious about his methods in promoting this 'Tractarian' agenda. He ruthlessly ousted the editor of a genteel high-church periodical, the *British Critic*, and transformed a hitherto staid and respectable magazine into a pugnacious mouthpiece of the new movement. He orchestrated an anonymous campaign of denigration and protest against the 'heretical' liberal theologian Renn Dickson Hamden, in an unsuccessful attempt to prevent his appointment as Regius Professor of Theology at Oxford in 1836. Such manoeuvrings showed Newman at his unattractive worst, and disgusted religious liberals like Thomas Arnold, the famous reforming headmaster of Rugby School, who branded Newman and his followers as 'the Oxford Malignants'. Ironically, Arnold's own sons were to fall under Newman's spell, and two of them would eventually follow him into the Catholic Church.

Newman's conviction that human nature needed redemption and divinization by incorporation into Christ put him utterly at odds with the utilitarian spirit that underlay much Victorian progressivism. Though himself a dedicated teacher, who spent his life promoting lay education in one form or another, he rejected entirely the idea that the increase of knowledge in itself brought moral improvement. In 1841 he wrote a brilliant series of satirical letters to the Times under the pseudonym *Catholicus*, attacking a speech Sir Robert Peel had made at the opening of a Library in Tamworth, in which Peel had said that as people improved their general knowledge by reading they 'rise at once in the scale of intellectual and moral existence, and feel the *moral dignity of his nature exalted*.' The pleasures of knowledge would overcome 'the indulgence of sensual appetite,' and help bring about 'the intellectual and *moral improvement* of the community.'

About all this Newman was magnificently scathing.

> … It does not require many words, … to determine that, taking human nature as it is actually found, and assuming that there is an Art of life, to say that it consists, or in any essential manner is placed, in the cultivation of Knowledge, that the mind is changed by a discovery, or saved by a diversion, and can thus be amused into immortality – that grief, anger, cowardice, self-conceit, pride, or passion, can be subdued by an examination of shells or grasses, or inhaling of gases, or chipping of rocks, or calculating the longitude, is the veriest of pretences which sophist or mountebank ever professed to a gaping auditory. If virtue be a mastery over the mind, if its end be action, if its perfection be inward order, harmony, and peace, we must

> seek it in graver and holier places than in Libraries and Reading-rooms.[6]

The Oxford Movement succeeded beyond its wildest expectations. In little over a generation it was to transform the theology, preaching, worship and even the architectural style of the Anglican Church: over the next century even conventionally middle-of-the-road parish churches were transformed from the preaching boxes of the eighteenth century into numinous settings for the celebration of ceremonial liturgy: village orchestras in the gallery gave way to surpliced choirs in the chancel, coloured stoles replaced black scarves, and Holy communion, once an occasional service happening four or five times a year, became a monthly or weekly event. Tractarianism was to be the single most important influence in the shaping of the character of the modern Anglican communion.

But by the early 1840s, Newman himself had lost confidence in it. He believed that the substantial teaching of the early church, and a 'Via Media' between the modern corruptions of the Church of Rome and the doctrinal and sacramental impoverishment of European Protestantism, were both to be found in the writings of Anglican high-churchmen like Lancelot Andrews or William Laud. But he rapidly came to recognize that this 'Via Media' had never been absorbed into main-stream Anglicanism: it was 'a paper theory', at odds with the visceral Protestantism and subjection to secular government of a national church. As he told the Irish high-churchman, Hugh James Rose, 'I cannot love the "Church of England" commonly so designated – its very title is an offence … for it implies that it holds, not of the Church Catholic but of the State.'[7]

Newman's increasingly subtle attempts to interpret the foundation documents of the Church of England in ways open to Roman Catholic teaching culminated in 1841 in the publication of Tract 90, which argued that subscription to the 39 Articles was compatible with holding Roman Catholic doctrines like the real presence of Christ in the bread and wine of the eucharist, or prayer for the dead. Tract 90 provoked a hostile backlash both from the bishops, and from older and more cautious high-churchmen. Frustrated by the apparently impregnable Protestantism of their contemporaries, one by one Newman's more headstrong disciples became Roman Catholics. Newman did what he could to stem the leakage, but the entirely predictable reaction to his Tract had deeply unsettled him, and he was himself in an agony of indecision, increasingly convinced that Rome possessed the fulness of truth, yet unable to bring his loyalties and emotions into accord with his intellect. 'Paper logic' was merely the trace of deeper and more mysterious movements of heart and mind. As he wrote later, recalling this long slow 'death-bed' as an Anglican, 'It is the concrete being that reasons: pass a number of years, and I find my mind in a new place; how? The whole man moves…Great acts take time.'[8] He retreated to Littlemore, part of St Mary's parish extending to the village near Oxford where he had built a church. There he and a dwindling band of followers lived a quasi-monastic life of prayer, fasting and reflection. In October 1845 Newman at last recognized where his own logic had long since led him, and he was received into the Roman Catholic Church.

Both Newman's attraction to Catholicism and his hesitation in embracing it sprang from a radical historicism. Historical criticism – of the Bible, of Christian institutions, of the evolution and transformations of Christian ideas

– was a major force for religious unsettlement in the nineteenth century. Newman was the first great theologian not merely to grasp the importance of the questions posed for faith by the fact of historical flux, but to insist that an acknowledgement of the historical contingency of much of Christian teaching and institutions was compatible with firmly held orthodox belief, with the acceptance of dogma. As an Anglican, he had begun by assuming that religious truth was unchanging. Christianity was a revealed religion, its doctrines descended to the present in an unbroken tradition from the Apostles. So nothing could count as Christian truth, unless the primitive church had believed and taught it. The modern Church of Rome, therefore, could not claim to be the true church, since so much about it – its elaborate ritualistic worship, the dominant place of the Virgin Mary in its piety, the overweening authority of the pope – all these seemed alien to or absent from the earliest Christianity: there were no rosary beads in third century Carthage. Yet Newman's reading in early Christian sources convinced him that to condemn Rome on these grounds would be to outlaw much of the rest of mainstream Christianity. The doctrines of Incarnation and Trinity, accepted as fundamental by both Catholics and Protestants, were not to be found in their mature form in the early church. And if the central tenets of the faith could develop legitimately beyond their New Testament foundations, why not everything else? As a Tractarian he dealt with this problem in part through the notion of a *disciplina arcana*, a secret tradition of doctrinal reticence – by which the early church had concealed or not spoken of fundamental beliefs in case they were profaned by scepticism or shallow belief: so there was an inner core of ancient beliefs not in scripture, but passed on to the initiated, and these doctrines in the course of time were openly articulated: they had always been there, just not in the written record.

Newman came to see the inadequacy of this essentially static and also highly speculative explanation. As Rowan Williams has pointed out, already in Newman's first book, his history of the *Arians of the Fourth Century* (1833) he had grasped that Christian doctrine evolved and changed, and to understand it we had to grasp the nature of that change.[9] To resolve the apparent contradiction between a religion of objectively revealed truth, and the manifest historical flux of Christian doctrines and practices, Newman wrote in his last years at Littlemore a theological masterpiece, the *Essay on the Development of Christian Doctrine* (1845). Its central claim is that the concepts and intuitions which shape human history are dynamic, not inert. Great ideas interact with changing times and cultures, retaining their distinctive thrust and direction, yet adapting so as to preserve and develop that energy in different circumstances. Truth is a plant, evolving from a seed into the mature tree, not a baton passed inertly from hand to hand. Ideas must unfold in the historical process before we can appropriate all that they contain. So beliefs evolve and change, but they do so to preserve their essence in the flux of history: they change, that is, in order to remain the same. 'In another world it is otherwise, but here below to live is to change, and to be perfect is to have changed often.'[10]

Other nineteenth century thinkers had anticipated aspects of this fundamentally dynamic understanding of religious truth. But no-one confronted its difficulties or explored its implications so fully as Newman, whose *Essay* offered a remarkable series of seven diagnostic tests by which to distinguish legitimate developments from corruptions of the truth. By no means everything in his analysis looks convincing now, but the *Essay* was a major intellectual landmark, and it legitimized the notion of doctrinal development, up till that point perceived as a weapon in the armoury of the unbeliever. Over the next century or so, it was to prove seminal for Catholic theology, as the Catholic Church increasingly sought to come to terms with its own historical contingency, and Newman's thinking has been equally influential in Protestant reflection on doctrinal development.

In the Catholic Church of the 1840s, however, Newman's brainwave was viewed with considerable suspicion. As the most famous clergyman in England, his was a prestigious scalp on the Pope's tentpole or, as he himself later complained, 'some wild incomprehensible beast caught by the hunter, and a spectacle for Dr Wiseman to exhibit to strangers...'[11]. For a while after his reordination as a Catholic priest, Rome treated him as a celebrity. But the nineteenth century Papacy was a beleaguered institution, its financial and political independence under threat from the movement for Italian unification, its ideological monopoly in European society everywhere challenged by the rise of often hostile modern nation states. Pope Pius IX reacted by denouncing modernity and emphasizing the Church's unchanging authority. In this atmosphere, Newman's nuanced historicism came to look half-hearted at best, treacherous at worst. He settled with a small group of devoted followers in Birmingham, as the founder and head of an English house of the Oratory of St Philip Neri, whom he adopted as his patron saint and model. But for almost twenty years after his conversion, frustration attended all he attempted, and his position within the Catholic Church became increasingly uncomfortable. An invitation to head a new Catholic University in Dublin elicited a sublime series of lectures on the nature of liberal education, published as *The Idea of a University*, hailed as a classic then, and a benchmark for liberal educational theorists ever since. Yet the project itself foundered amidst considerable bitterness, the casualty in part of Newman's own difficult personality, his competing projects and preoccupations, and of the mismatch between his desire to create a blueprint for Christian education for anglophone Catholics, and the hard-headed pragmatism of the Irish bishops, intent on rebuilding a nation decimated by Famine. They were not looking for an idealized Catholic Oxford, but an institute of practical education for an aspiring Catholic Irish middle class.

Back in England, Newman yearned for an Oratorian mission to Oxford itself, and a return to the university which he loved and in which he had once thrived. He bought land for a church and house there, but the Catholic bishops feared that exposure to the flesh-pots of the establishment would lure Catholic undergraduates into apostasy. The Vatican too, beleaguered in secularizing Italy and fighting a rearguard action to defend the Church's traditional monopoly on education, was increasingly jumpy about Catholic attendance at non-Catholic schools and universities. So Newman's Oxford project was blocked, not least by his erstwhile friend, Henry Edward Manning, future cardinal, and now an implacably papalist Catholic zealot. Newman's own orthodoxy became suspect. In an essay in the liberal Catholic journal *The Rambler*, whose editorship he had reluctantly accepted in order to prevent its closure by the bishops, he defended the notion that the laity were not passive recipients of clerical teaching, the *ecclesia discens*, the learning or listening church, subordinate to the *ecclesia docens*, the hierarchical teaching church, but were themselves witnesses to and transmitters of

Catholic truth. Yet in Pio Nono's (Pope Pius IX) church, the only role expected of the laity was to listen, obey and cough up for collections. To suggest otherwise was a charter for insubordination. Newman was delated to Rome for heresy, and there were abortive attempts to extract a recantation from the man whom Mgr George Talbot, a hugely influential Papal adviser and once an admirer, now called 'the most dangerous man in England.'

Unsurprisingly, Newman, always prone to self-pity, felt increasingly isolated and abandoned, conscious that the influence he had exerted as an Anglican had melted away from the moment he had converted, aware of the haggard lines which disappointment had etched into his face, bitter that all his endeavours seemed to 'crumble under my hands, as if one were making ropes of sand.'[12] He was rescued at the end of 1863 by a casually anti-Catholic journal article by the novelist Charles Kingsley, who remarked in passing that truth had never been considered a virtue by Catholic clergy, and that Newman in particular had proposed 'cunning' as the weapon given to the Church 'to withstand the brute male force of the wicked world.' This unprovoked attack on his integrity, not to mention its snide insinuation about his manhood, was the trigger for Newman's best-known and most beautiful book, his *Apologia Pro Vita Sua*, written for serial publication at breakneck speed, in just ten weeks. Years of unhappy brooding over his own religious journey, and of sorting and annotating his correspondence, proved ideal preparation for the writing of a religious autobiography which is also a triumphant self-vindication, one of the most persuasive portrayals of a mind and heart in movement in English or any other language. Overnight, Newman's embrace of what to many had seemed an exotic and alien religion was made intelligible to Victorian readers. Catholics hailed him as a brilliant apologist who presented their unpopular religion in a new and sympathetic light: Anglicans remembered that this man had once transformed the established church for the better. Newman had become an Eminent Victorian.

It's worth emphasizing that the *Apologia* was both more and less than an autobiography: it was a highly selective account of his intellectual journey towards Catholicism, not a general history of his life as an Anglican, though recent attempts to interpret it as a brilliant confidence trick concealing his true opinions, seem crassly wrong-headed. Its final part was also a manifesto not only for his kind of Catholicism, but also for his understanding of the nature of Christianity itself, which extended the austere vision of the Parochial and Plain sermons in an analysis of the human condition as sombre and as profound as that of Dostoyevsky.

> To consider the world in its length and breadth, its various history, the many races of man, their starts, their fortunes, their mutual alienation, their conflicts; and then their ways, habits, governments, forms of worship; their enterprises, their aimless courses, their random achievements and acquirements, the impotent conclusion of long-standing facts, the tokens so faint and broken[,] of a superintending design, the blind evolution of what turn out to be great powers or truths, the progress of things, as if from unreasoning elements, not towards final causes, the greatness and littleness of man, his far-reaching aims, his short duration, the curtain hung over his futurity, the disappointments of life, the defeat of good, the success of evil, physical pain, mental anguish, the prevalence and intensity of sin, the pervading idolatries, the corruptions,

> the dreary hopeless irreligion, that condition of the whole race, so fearfully yet exactly described in the Apostle's words, "having no hope and without God in the world – all this is a vision to dizzy and appal; and inflicts upon the mind the sense of a profound mystery, which is absolutely beyond human solution.[13]

His fame gave him leverage – and a degree of immunity – within Pio Nono's church, but it didn't reconcile him to the direction that church was taking. Manning, who succeeded Nicholas Wiseman as Archbishop of Westminster in 1865, was deeply distrustful of what he saw as the compromised and compromising minimalism of Newman's Catholicism, which he criticized as 'always on the lower side… the old, Anglican, patristic, literary, Oxford tone transplanted into the Church.'[14] And the tide of events was with Manning. Newman watched with dismay the progress of an exaggerated papalism which he thought distorted and undermined the Church's credibility. In January 1870 he wrote an angry letter to his bishop, which was later sensationally leaked to the press, in which he denounced the pressure for the definition of papal infallibility

> When we are all at rest, and have no doubts, and at least practically, not to say doctrinally, hold the Holy Father to be infallible, suddenly there is thunder in the clear sky, and we are told to prepare for something we know not what to try our faith we know not how. No impending danger is to be averted, but a great difficulty is to be created. Is this the proper work for an Ecumenical Council? As to myself personally, please God, I do not expect any trial at all; but I cannot help suffering with the various souls which are suffering, and I look with anxiety at the prospect of having

> to defend decisions, which may be not difficult to my private judgment, but may be most difficult to maintain logically in the face of historical facts. What have we done to be treated, as the faithful never were treated before? When has definition of doctrine *de fide* been a luxury of devotion, and not a stern painful necessity? Why should an agressive insolent faction be allowed to 'make the heart of the just to mourn, whom the Lord hath not made sorrowful?' Why can't we be let alone, when we have pursued peace, and thought no evil?[15]

This kind of utterance did nothing to gain Newman friends at Rome, but he was not deterred. He had in fact mounted his own single-handed campaign to sabotage the new ultramontanism, by presenting an alternative face of Catholicism. In a series of works ostensibly designed to defend the Church against its external critics, he undermined the authoritarian and clericalist Catholicism being promoted by Manning and his associates. In the process, he subtly redrew the lines of contemporary religious debate, and sketched what was to prove to be the future of Catholic theology. A reply in 1866 to his old Anglican colleague Edward Bouverie Pusey, defending the Catholic veneration of the Virgin, recentred Marian doctrine by insisting that all that was essential in it was already present in the teaching of the Greek and Latin Fathers: this at once sidelined the baroque elaborations of modern Italian mariology which the head of the 'breakaway' London Oratory, Fr Frederick William Faber, was ardently promoting. In a reply to Gladstone's hysterical denunciations of the likely effects of the Vatican Council on Catholic allegiance to secular rulers, Newman set clear limits to Papal authority, disparaged by contrast the extremism of Ultramontanes like Manning and Newman's former disciple W. G. Ward, and (famously) pledged a toast to 'conscience first, and the Pope afterwards.' A new *Preface* to his own Anglican writing on ecclesiology subverted the authoritarianism of Pio Nono's pontificate by arguing that critical theology, spiritual life or piety, and hierarchical (especially papal) authority, were each indispensable functions or 'offices' of the Church, but were permanently in dialectical tension. Catholic truth, he argued, was distorted whenever any one of these three offices gained the upper hand over the others, as, by implication, hierarchy had in his own day.

Newman's *Preface* to the 1877 reissue of the *Lectures on the Prophetical Office of the Church* was his last great original theological work. Throughout the 1860s and 70s he was engaged in a systematic reissue of his Anglican writings, a self-conscious assertion of the integrity and consistency of his own intellectual and spiritual journey. What eventually became a uniform edition of all his writings was designed to establish the essential Catholicity of ideas gestated during his Anglican years, many of which, unsurprisingly, were viewed with suspicion by hyper-Catholics like Manning and Ward. This was a tricky venture in the Church of Pio Nono, and it's typical of Newman that his highly original final exercise in ecclesiology should present itself as something ostensibly quite different, an apologetic defence of the Catholic Church of the 1870s against the accusations of the fierce young Anglican high-churchman he had been in the 1840s.

Newman's later writings were not confined to the internal affairs of the Church. In 1870, in the midst of the furore over papal infallibility, he published his most sustained philosophical work, the *Grammar of Assent*. It's an austere and difficult book, taking up and developing ideas which had been first aired in his *Oxford University Sermons*, published in 1843. The *Grammar* was a searching exploration of the nature and motives of religious belief: some of its central themes were already familiar in (and quoted from) his Anglican writings: in *The Tamworth Reading Room* he had insisted on the personal nature of our apprehension of truth, and the inadequacy of logic as a basis for life-changing beliefs.

> Logic makes but a sorry rhetoric with the multitude; first shoot round corners, and you may not despair of converting by a syllogism. Few men have that power of mind which may hold fast and firmly a variety of thoughts. … To most men argument makes the point in hand only more doubtful, and considerably less impressive. After all, man is not a reasoning animal; he is a seeing, feeling, contemplating, acting animal. …
>
> Life is not long enough for a religion of inferences; we shall never have done beginning, if we determine to begin with proof. We shall ever be laying our foundations... Resolve to believe nothing, and you must prove your proofs and analyze your elements, sinking further and further, and finding "in the lowest depth a lower deep," till you come to the broad bosom of scepticism. I would rather be bound to defend the reasonableness of assuming that Christianity is true, than to demonstrate a moral governance from the physical world. Life is for action. If we insist on proofs for everything, we shall never come to action: to act you must assume, and that assumption is faith.[16]

The *Grammar of Assent* teases out in detail the implications of that view of faith as a venture: it took him twenty years to write, and the Oxford philosopher, Sir Anthony Kenny, has described it as the most significant contribution to epistemology between Descartes and Wittgenstein.[17] In it, Newman's hostility to 'liberalism', the rationalist reduction to mere 'paper logic' of the processes by which we make life and death decisions, finds its most powerful expression. His subtle analysis of the sometimes untraceable routes by which we arrive at conviction, the 'personal conquest of truth', anticipates some of the later Wittgenstein's characteristic positions, though it is not clear that Wittgenstein ever read *The Grammar of Assent*.

The frustrations and disappointments of Newman's Catholic career had not ended with the publication of the *Apologia*: Archbishop Manning saw to it that he was never permitted to re-establish himself at Oxford. But the renewal of Anglican friendships which the *Apologia* enabled, the national celebrity it revived, and the Catholic gratitude which it elicited help explain the renewal of energy and purpose which underlay his last writings. With the death of Pio Nono in February 1878, his standing as the leading English exponent of Catholic faith would be vindicated. Early in 1879, at the prompting of the Duke of Norfolk, Newman's friend and former pupil at Newman's Oratory School, the new pope, Leo XIII, agreed to offer Newman the red hat of a cardinal. Newman, afraid that he would be required to leave Birmingham and live in the Curia at Rome, wrote an uncharacteristically tortuous letter pleading not to be removed from 'my little nest'. Manning, who privately believed Newman to be a heretic, chose to interpret this letter as a refusal, informed the Pope accordingly, and spread word that Newman had declined the Pope's offer. Only urgent interventions by the Duke of Norfolk and Bishop Ullathorne of Birmingham resolved the misunderstanding, if such it was. Manning backtracked, loudly protested a genuine mistake, and Dr Newman became Cardinal Newman. He told his Oratorians, 'The cloud is lifted from me forever', and to his Anglican friend Richard Church he wrote

> all the stories which have gone about of my being a half Catholic, a liberal Catholic, under a cloud, not to be trusted, are now at an end. Poor Ward can no longer call me a heretic …[18].

Newman combined a life-long insistence on the reliability of revealed truth – of dogma – with a vivid awareness of the contingency of all Christian understanding and utterance, even the most solemn creeds. In his consequent exploration of the legitimacy of the development of doctrine: in his rejection of a narrow enlightenment understanding of rationality: in his recognition of the puzzle and difficulty of belief in God while simultaneously defending the reasonableness of religious commitment; in his understanding of the dynamic nature of the institutional church, the impossibility of neat and tidy harmonizations of the competing demands of truth, power and intuition, and our consequent need and ability to live with the inevitable tensions between them; in his rejection of exaggerated claims for religious authority and his insistence on the role and dignity of the laity even in the sphere of faith, Newman identified and explored many of the issues which would most preoccupy theology in the twentiethcentury. Every other Victorian theologian has become of mainly historical interest. Newman's writings are still worth reading for their continuing relevance and vitality. He is still our contemporary.

2
Newman and the Fathers

Throughout his long life, Newman's imagination was fired by the study of the first Christian centuries. Paradoxically, his greatest originality as a thinker sprang from that imaginative engagement with the distant past. Already, in the first flush of his evangelical conversion at the age of fifteen, he was 'nothing short of enamoured' by the long extracts from St Augustine, St Ambrose and others he encountered in the pages of Joseph Milner's *Church History*. From 1828 he began reading the Greek Fathers systematically, and he felt 'set up in the patristical line' when, three years later, a group of friends and former pupils presented him with a multi-volume set of the best modern editions of most of the major early church writers. From the outset, Newman's scholarly exploration of Christian antiquity was never purely academic: he looked to 'the primitive church' as a mirror and pattern for the present, 'the true exponent of the doctrines of Christianity and the basis of the Church of England.'[19]

As the Oxford Movement confronted in the early 1830s what seemed the withdrawal of the state's support for the Church's privileged status, he appealed (somewhat improbably, and perhaps mischievously) to the example of fourth century bishops like St Ambrose or St Athanasius defying heretical Emperors and Empresses, as the pattern for the contemporary English episcopate confronted by reforming Whig governments: as he wrote in the first of the Tracts for the *Times*, 'Thoughts on the Ministerial Commission',

> black event as it would be for the country, yet, (as far as [the bishops] are concerned,) we could not wish them a more blessed termination of their course, than the spoiling of their goods, and martyrdom.[20]

In the summer of 1833 he began the first of a series of popular magazine articles on early church themes, which he later collected into a book entitled *The Church of the Fathers*, overtly designed to stiffen resistance to the erosion of the Church's place in English society and, less overtly, to accustom nineteenth century Anglicans to 'Apostolical' ideas on church, doctrine, sacraments, and the religious and ascetical life. In his 1837 *Lectures on The Prophetical Office of the Church*, Newman's most coherent articulation of the idea of Anglicanism as a *Via Media* between 'Roman and Protestant errors', he would argue that 'whatever doctrine … may fairly and reasonably be considered to be the universal belief of those ages, is to be received as coming from the Apostles … Catholicity, Antiquity, and consent of Fathers, is the proper evidence of the fidelity or Apostolicity of a professed Tradition.'[21] A growing realization of the problems inherent in measuring the vitality or legitimacy of any existing Christian body by this essentially static notion of Christian authenticity would lead him to the idea of doctrinal development, and ultimately to identify the modern Church of Rome, rather than the Church of England as the legitimate continuation of the Church of the Fathers.

Newman's first book-length exploration of Christian antiquity, *The Arians of the Fourth Century*, appeared in

November 1833. Originally commissioned as part of a series providing background to the Thirty-Nine Articles, *Arians* evolved into something radically different, a study of the great Christological battles of the fourth century, which Newman saw as paradigms for the perennial struggle to articulate the mystery of God faithfully to a hostile or uncomprehending world. Notoriously, *Arians* is marred by a 'colossally over-schematic' contrast between the 'true' Christian tradition of Alexandria – mystical, poetic, sensitive to the metaphorical dimensions of scripture and of all discourse about God – and the false theology in vogue in ancient Antioch, which Newman considered aridly rationalist, literal and reductively historicist, the type of a theology 'dictated by human wisdom, human desire, and reluctance to be humble before revelation.'[22] He argued, unconvincingly, that although Arius was an Alexandrian priest, the heresy that bore his name was the offspring of Antiochine (and behind that, Jewish) rationalism. Newman's account of these fourth century debates is coloured by sometimes forced parallels to the religious parties of his own day: the favour shown to Arianism by successive emperors is likened to court patronage of nineteenth century whig churchmen, while his chapter on the Eclectic sect claimed to find in this ancient philosophy 'the chief features of that recent school of liberalism and false illumination, political and moral, which is now Satan's instrument in deluding the nations ... the cold, scoffing spirit of modern rationalism.'[23]

Yet historically questionable as Newman's contrast between Antiochine and Alexandrian theology was, his immersion in the writings of the Alexandrian Fathers from Clement and Origen to Athanasius was foundational for his own understanding of the nature and limits of Christian theology, and contained the seeds of his own later thinking about doctrinal development. As he was to recall in the *Apologia*,

> Some portions of their teaching, magnificent in themselves, came like music to my inward ear … . These were based on the mystical or sacramental principle … I understood them to mean that the exterior world, physical and historical, was but the outward manifestation to our senses of realities greater than itself. Nature was a parable: Scripture was an allegory: pagan literature, philosophy, and mythology, properly understood, were but a preparation for the Gospel. The Greek poets and sages were in a certain sense prophets; for "thoughts beyond their thought to those high bards were given." There had been a directly divine dispensation granted to the Jews … first one disclosure and then another, till the whole evangelical doctrine was brought into full manifestation. And thus room was made for the anticipation of further and deeper disclosures, of truths still under the veil of the letter, and in their season to be revealed. The visible world still remains without its divine interpretation; Holy Church in her sacraments and her hierarchical appointments, will remain even to the end of the world, only a symbol of those heavenly facts which fill eternity. Her mysteries are but the expressions in human language of truths to which the human mind is unequal.[24]

Given Newman's hounding of doctrinal liberalizers like Professor Hamden, and his own lifelong insistence that creeds and dogmatic definitions were essential to preserve the apostolic witness, that emphasis on the centrality of symbol and metaphor in religious discourse, and the ultimate inadequacy of credal language to the realities it proclaims, were among the most remarkable features of *Arians*. He argued that even necessary dogmatic formulations represented a tragic diminishment, true as far as they went but always the reduction of ineffable mysteries to the 'technicality and formalism' of formulae too small to contain them. In credal definition, he wrote, 'we count the words of the Fathers, and measure their sentences; and so convert doxologies into creeds. That we do so … is the fault of those who have obliged us, of those who, "while men slept", have "sowed tares among the wheat".'[25] Heresy demands rebuttal: but freedom from such definitions 'is abstractedly the highest state of Christian communion', because

> when confessions do not exist, the mysteries of divine truth, instead of being exposed to the gaze of the profane and uninstructed, are kept hidden in the bosom of the Church, far more faithfully than is otherwise possible.

Dogmatic declarations 'most true as they are, still are daily wrested by infidels to their ruin', and give rise to the 'mischievous fanaticism' of those who imagine

> that they can explain the sublime doctrines and exuberant promises of the Gospel, before they have yet learned to know themselves and to discern the holiness of God, under the preparatory discipline of the Law and of Natural Religion.[26]

That last sentence was a sideswipe at contemporary evangelicals, whose preaching in Newman's view crassly exposed the mysteries of atonement and predestination to irreverent and unprepared listeners. Yet his underlying belief that doctrinal definition was always a tragic necessity forced on a reluctant Church by the challenge of heresy would remain a core conviction. It accounts for his indignation in 1870 against the 'aggressive, insolent faction' campaigning for the definition of papal infallibility, when 'no impending danger is to be averted, but a great difficulty is to be created', thereby turning definition of doctrine *de fide* into 'a luxury of devotion, and not a stern painful necessity.'[27]

Newman's reflections on the problems of dogmatic definition rose out of his study of the Christological beliefs of pre-Nicene authors, whose language on the subordination of Christ to God the Father was difficult to square with later Conciliar definitions. Anglican writers like the seventeenth century theologian-bishop George Bull, on whose work Newman drew heavily, had approached this problem essentially a-historically, insisting or assuming that the pre-Nicene church, all appearances to the contrary, had in fact consciously held the full post-Nicene teaching, and Bull had read third century texts in the light of later formulations. Newman knew that judged by post-Nicene criteria, the earliest christian writers looked like heretics, and his extended discussion of the origins of Trinitarian doctrine in *Arians* show that he was alert to the historical problems in assuming identity between their teaching and later Catholic orthodoxy: he was aware that doctrine had a history. To that extent, *Arians* represented a new and more critical approach to patristic study. But at this stage he located the solution to the difficulty mainly in the almost equally a-historical notion of a *disciplina arcan*a, a rule of secrecy by which the early church avoided committing the most sacred doctrines to writing or public disclosure, instead revealing them progressively in catechesis and liturgy as neophytes matured in their faith. Nevertheless, *Arians*, for all its flaws, unmistakeably laid the groundwork for Newman's most original and abiding theological legacy, and opened a line of enquiry whose most momentous outcome would be the *Essay on Development*.

Newman's engagement with Alexandrian theology pervaded his own original theological thinking. This is most obvious in the 1838 *Lectures on Justification*, which moved beyond the stale oppositional categories of 'Romanist and Protestant' that had dogged the subject since the sixteenth century, by locating Justification primarily neither in faith or works alone, but in divine self-communication through the Holy Spirit, and the consequent divinization of human nature. The remarkable emphasis in the lectures on the Holy Spirit as the agent in Christ's resurrection and as the medium of his indwelling in us as a glorified and justifying presence, introduced a visionary Christological ardour into his exposition that was exceedingly rare in Victorian theologizing:

> It would seem, moreover, as I have said, that He has done so by ascending to the Father; that His ascent bodily is His descent spiritually; that His taking our nature up to God, is the descent of God into us; that He has truly, though in an unknown sense, taken us to God, or brought down God to us, according as we view it Thus, when St. Paul says that our life is hid with Him in God, we may suppose him to intimate that our principle of existence is no longer a mortal, earthly principle, such as Adam's after his fall, but that we are baptized and hidden anew in God's glory, in that Shekinah of light and purity which we lost when Adam fell – that we are new-created, transformed, spiritualized, glorified in the Divine Nature – that through the participation of Christ, we receive, as through a channel, the true Presence of God within and without us, imbuing us with sanctity and

> immortality. *This*, I repeat, is our justification, our ascent through Christ to God, or God's descent through Christ to us; we may call it either of the two; we ascend into Him, He descends into us; we are in Him, He in us; Christ being the One Mediator, the way, the truth, and the life, joining earth with heaven.[28]

Alexandrian influence was similarly responsible for some of the most radiant and uplifting passages in Newman's preaching, but it could also startle and bemuse. Notoriously, his Christology was dauntingly exalted, and one can only wonder what congregations used to addressing 'Gentle Jesus, meek and mild' would have made of this utterance, in April 1836:

> though He was in nature perfect man, He was not man in exactly the same sense in which any one of us is a man. Though man, He was not, strictly speaking, in the English sense of the word, a man; He was not such as one of us, and one out of a number. … His incarnation was a "taking of the manhood into God." As He had no earthly father, so has He no human personality. We may not speak of Him as we speak of any individual man, acting from and governed by a human intelligence within Him, but He was God, acting not only as God, but now through the flesh also, when He would. He was not a man made God, but God made man.[29]

Newman's conviction that the Church of England was 'substantially founded' on the Fathers led to his cooperation with Pusey in the establishment of the *Library of the Fathers*, publishing translations of the major theologians of the early church. He was very conscious of potential resistance to the project, given the "startling" unfamiliarity of much patristic teaching to Protestant sensibilities. In the preface to his edition of the *Catechetical lectures of St Cyril of Jerusalem* he conceded that the Fathers were 'witnesses to Apostolic truth not individually but collectively … no one of the Fathers is necessarily right in all his doctrine, taken by himself, but may be erroneous in secondary points, [and] in danger, by his own peculiarities … of throwing discredit on all together … .'[30]

The question of which modern church had the best claim to teach the Catholic 'fundamentals' represented by the consensus of the Fathers was the issue at the heart of Newman's 1837 *Lectures on the Prophetical Office of the Church*, Newman's most important exposition of the *Via Media*. The lectures were in large part an anti-Protestant polemic, 'hitting the Peculiars [Evangelicals] a most uncommon blow in the face.'[31] Yet they were just as obviously a sustained attack on the Roman Catholic Church for its alleged corruption of the fundamental teaching of the ancient church as distilled into the ancient Creeds. So Newman had to provide a rationale for the fact that every church, including the Church of England, expected from its adherents far more than subscription to the creeds, or what he calls the 'Episcopal tradition' of formally defined doctrine derived from the Apostles (which he believed to be infallible). With striking originality, he suggested that there was also a subordinate but still authoritative 'Prophetic tradition', which represented a legitimate outworking of those fundamental beliefs. If the Apostles and after them the bishops were the authoritative sources of the Church's teaching, Prophets were the *interpreters* of revelation; 'they unfold and define its mysteries, they illuminate its documents, they harmonize its contents, they apply its promises.' But this unfolding was no mere expository exercise, to be gleaned from the works of long dead clergymen. Unlike the Episcopal tradition, which was lodged primarily in solemn formularies and authoritative teachers and rulers, namely the bishops, the Prophetic tradition was a far more diffuse and elusive reality. It was

> a vast system … consisting of a certain body of Truth, permeating the Church like an atmosphere, irregular in its shape from its very profusion and exuberance: at times separable only in idea from Episcopal Tradition, yet at times melting away into legend and fable; partly written, partly unwritten, partly the interpretation, partly the supplement of Scripture, partly preserved in intellectual expressions, partly latent in the spirit and temper of Christians; poured to and fro in closets and upon the housetops, in liturgies, in controversial works, in obscure fragments, in sermons… existing primarily in the bosom of the Church itself, and recorded in such measure as providence has determined in the writings of eminent men.

Though by its nature fallible and more susceptible than the Episcopal Tradition to corruption and abuse, this Prophetic Tradition also deserved the 'dutiful and simple-hearted acceptance' of the Church's children.[32]

With many loose ends and unresolved questions, in this distinction between what gave the Church form – the episcopal tradition – and what gave it life – the prophetic tradition – Newman was manifestly reaching here towards an extraordinarily rich understanding of Christian tradition that in some ways anticipates the teaching of the Second Vatican Council's Dogmatic Constitution on Revelation, *Dei Verbum*. Significantly, the phrase 'in the bosom of the Church', which he had deployed in *Arians* to characterize the Church's cherishing of divine truth before the challenge of heresy forced it into formal definition, is applied here to the whole 'Prophetic tradition'. This highlights the difficulty Newman had in maintaining a sharp distinction between the so called 'fundamentals', and the more diffuse and fallible outworking or embodiment of those fundamentals in the life of the Church: that ambiguity would edge him towards the idea of the development of doctrine: it also anticipates elements of the analysis of the threefold energies within the Church in his remarkable *Preface* to the 1877 edition of The *Via Media*.[33]

Up to this point, the study of the early church had served to bolster Newman's confidence in the Anglican Church. Thereafter, it began to tug him towards Rome. The summer of 1839 represented a decisive stage in this shift. After four years when other preoccupations had halted his patristic studies, he found himself almost alone in Oriel and able to resume what he called 'my own line of reading'. And 'it was during this course of reading that for the first time a doubt came upon me of the tenableness of Anglicanism.'[34] He had turned his attention to the Monophysite controversies of the fifth century on the nature of the union of divine and human in Christ, and the doctrinal settlement of the Council of Chalcedon. Always on the alert for parallels between the history of the early church and that of the present day, Newman began to question whether Christian truth after all would be found in a 'Via Media' between supposed extremes. For the records seemed to suggest that the Monophysite Oriental churches had presented themselves as moderates seeking compromise, and it was the Pope then who repudiated compromise: yet it was the Pope's teaching that had been vindicated by the Council. As Newman recalled in the *Apologia*, 'My stronghold was Antiquity: now … I saw my face in that mirror, and I was a Monophysite.'[35]

Worse was to follow, in September a friend drew his attention to an article on 'The Anglican Claim to Apostolical Succession' by Nicholas Wiseman, in the August issue of the Roman Catholic *Dublin Review*, in the course of which Wiseman compared modern Anglicanism to the Donatist schism in fourth century North Africa. Newman at first dismissed the article, but his friend pointed to a sentence of St Augustine's cited by Wiseman, *Securus judicat orbis terrarum*: 'the judgement of the whole world is to be trusted'. Newman of course did not believe in truth by referendum: he knew that in the Arian controversy a majority of bishops had fallen into heresy. But here was a criterion of truth 'simpler than that of Antiquity', indeed 'Antiquity declaring against itself'. What was being claimed, with what seemed to him devastating plausibility, was that 'the deliberate judgement in which the whole church at length rests and acquiesces, is an infallible prescription and a final sentence against such portions of it as protest and secede.' By Augustine's words, it now seemed to him, 'the theory of the *Via Media* was absolutely pulverized.'[36]

It was a turning point. To calm his own doubts and those of his followers, he published a long article in the *British Critic* in January 1840 on the *Catholicity of the Anglican Church*, 'my last arrow against Rome', conceding that the Church of England claimed to be part of the Catholic Church while being out of communion with the rest of that Church, both east and west, but arguing that 'Augustine's maxim about submission to the *orbis terrarum* ... is a presumption rather than a law.' Anglicans were like the semi-Arians in the time of St Basil, who, though visibly separated 'from the general body' of the Church, were nevertheless, sufficiently 'sound in faith' and holiness of life to be considered in communion 'with the invisible church.'[37] Newman would continue to deploy special pleading of this sort for another four years,[38] but as he confided to a horrified Henry Wilberforce, 'a vista has been opened before me, to the end of which I do not see.'[39]

The end of that vista was, of course, his reception into the Church of Rome in October 1845, but an immense obstacle had first to be removed. Newman identified true Christianity with the church of the early centuries, but the passage of eighteen centuries meant that no modern institution seemed straightforwardly identical with the Church of the Fathers, Protestantism least of all, with its deliberate renunciation of most of the Christian past as a history of corruption, and its attempt to refound Christianity on the Bible alone. 'Whatever be historical Christianity', he considered, 'it is not Protestantism … To be deep in history is to cease to be a Protestant.'[40] Yet the Roman Catholic Church of the mid nineteenth century, with its centralized papacy, its baroque churches and liturgy, its lavish devotion to the Virgin, seemed at first sight very remote indeed from Primitive Christianity. Here seemed an insuperable difficulty. Now, as he was increasingly convinced that Rome in the end 'would be found to be right', he needed a hypothesis that would account for this difficulty. That hypothesis was the idea of the development of doctrine.

Newman had sketched the outlines of a theory of development as early as November 1840 in a letter to his brother Frank, who rejected as corruption all development beyond what was explicit in the New Testament. By contrast, Newman maintained 'All systems which have life, have a development, yet do not cease to have an identity though they develop.' By development at this point he meant 'the more accurate statement and the varied application of ideas from the action of the reason upon them according to new circumstances.' The criteria he sketched for assessing authentic developments were essentially reducible to internal consistency and discernible continuity with the original revelation. The characterization of such historical consistency he suggested to Frank was calculated to challenge, even to startle, as much as to convince: 'the temper and principles of the Church have been precisely the same from first to last, from the Apostolic age to this; viz what her enemies call dogmatic, mystical, credulous, superstitious, bigotted, legal.'[41] Newman made a more developed, but also more limited, attempt at articulating a theory in a university sermon preached in February 1843, on the text 'Mary kept all these things, and pondered them in her heart'. Taking a lead from the text, his account of development in the sermon was essentially psychological: he compared the authentic development of doctrine to the slow teasing out of an inchoate, but real apprehension, as intuitions and ideas 'latent in the Christian mind' were made explicit as they were reflected upon, and their implications slowly explored.[42]

In the *Essay on Development*, which Newman began writing in March 1845, he would elaborate that insight, but recast the argument in much broader historical terms: 'from the nature of the human mind, time is necessary for the full comprehension and perfection of great ideas.'[43] But this process is not the mere logical exposition of a deep thought:

> The development … of an idea is not like an investigation worked out on paper, in which each successive advance is a pure evolution from a foregoing, but it is carried on through and by means of communities of men and their leaders and guides; and it employs their minds as its instruments, and depends upon them, while it uses them"[44]

A living 'idea' generates and responds to complex social and historical energies, whose outworkings have a capacity to surprise – its beginnings 'are no measure of its capabilities, nor of its scope', for

> the more claim an idea has to be considered living, the more various will be its aspects; and the more social and political is its nature, the more complicated and subtle will be its issues, and the longer and more eventful will be its course . . .[45]

But these transformations are not signs of instability: on the contrary, they are designed to conserve the integrity of the idea in changing circumstances: the idea changes, 'in order to remain the same'.

So how are we to be certain the idea has indeed remained the same: what distinguished an authentic development from a corruption or betrayal? Newman proposed seven 'tests' of a genuine development. These were (1) 'Preservation of type' – the maintenance of the integrity of the original idea despite significant change. (2) 'Continuity of principles' – fidelity to the core ideas of Christianity, such as the Incarnational or sacramental principle. (3) 'Power of assimilation' – an example (not Newman's) might be the way in which medieval Christianity was able to assimilate an 'alien' philosophical system – Aristotelianism – to its own purposes. (4) 'Logical sequence': although developments do not proceed from strict deduction, retrospectively the logical coherence of the development that has actually occurred will be recognizable. (5) 'Anticipation of its future': true developments emerge from hints already present, even if only minimally and vaguely, as the cult of relics is derived from the belief in the resurrection of the body: (6)

'Conservative action on its past'; true developments clarify and corroborate earlier elements, whereas a corruption corrects or changes them. (7) 'Chronic vigour' – true developments have lasting power and the ability to flourish, corruptions and heresies wither away.[46]

These so-called 'tests' were of course every bit as impressionistic and subjective as those outlined in Newman's 1840 letter to his brother Frank, and when he came to revise the *Essay* he rearranged them and called them 'Notes' rather than 'tests', indicating that they were general characteristics rather than objective criteria of a truthful development.[47] Newman was not unduly concerned by their inconclusiveness: he believed that in an infallible Church, God had provided an ultimate judge of authentic developments, and he included a chapter arguing for the reasonableness or 'antecedent probability' of such an 'infallible arbitration'. That emphasis was integral to Newman's insistence that an authentic development must be known to be true to the original revelation. Yet it also reflected his very distinctive concern to emphasize the role of the whole of the Church in the process of discernment: as he told John Acton, 'I should like to say that the Church apprehends it more clearly … When I suggested it to Fr Perrone, he disliked the idea – but what is the Church as separate from Pope, Councils, Bishops, and faithful?'[48]

These tests or notes have always been among the most controversial and least satisfactory aspects of the *Essay*: but they are not its centre. The heart of the book is the three chapters offered as applications of the first test and 'Illustrations of the argument in behalf of the existing developments of Christianity'. These surveyed in turn the christianity of the 'first centuries', the fourth century, and the fifth and sixth centuries, each chapter a *tour de force* offering a vivid broad-brush characterization of the Church in that age, and each culminating in a final paragraph that finds the same characteristics in modern Roman Catholicism. As always, the examples are designed to challenge a Protestant readership as much as to persuade. So, his survey of the fourth century emphasizes the struggle to assert and maintain orthodoxy and the unity and authority of the Catholic Church in the face of Arianism and other heresies, and then concludes:

> On the whole, then, we have reason to say, that if there be a form of Christianity at this day distinguished for its careful organization, and its consequent power; if it is spread over the world; if it is conspicuous for zealous maintenance of its own creed; if it is intolerant towards what it considers error; if it is engaged in ceaseless war with all other bodies called Christian; if it, and it alone, is called 'Catholic' by the world, nay, by those very bodies, and if it makes much of the title; if it names them heretics, and warns them of coming woe, and calls on them one by one, to come over to itself, overlooking every other tie; and if they, on the other hand, call it seducer, harlot, apostate, Antichrist, devil; if, however much they differ one with another, they consider it their common enemy; if they strive to unite together against it, and cannot; if they are but local; if they continually subdivide, and it remains one; if they fall one after another, and make way for new sects, and it remains the same; such a religious communion is not unlike historical Christianity, as it comes before us at the Nicene Era.[49]

This is not a form of argument calculated to convince a hostile sceptic, but that was not its purpose. Newman wrote the *Essay* to remove the remaining obstacles he himself had felt to identification of the Church of Gregory XVI with the Church of Athanasius and Leo the Great: before he had finished the book his doubts had disappeared. On 9 October 1845, in his 'monastery' at Littlemore, he was received into the Roman Catholic Church by the Italian Passionist missionary, Fr (now Blessed) Dominic Barberi, and the *Essay* was published it as it stood, incomplete.

Newman was well aware that he had opened a line of enquiry, not said the last word on it. As he told H. J. Coleridge, his theory was 'characterized by incompleteness and crudeness – but it is something to have started a problem, and mapped in part a country, if I have done nothing more.'[50] No one, then or since, has found all aspects of his argument satisfactory, and he himself was prone at times to minimize its range and novelty – as he wrote to the future Lord Acton in 1862, 'to me the words "development in dogma" are substantially nothing but the process by which, under the magisterium of the Church, implicit faith becomes explicit.'[51] But every subsequent discussion of development of doctrine has had to engage with Newman's *Essay*. For the first time a major Christian thinker had confronted head-on the radical contingency of Christianity as an historical phenomenon, had acknowledged that doctrine, ritual and church organization all change over time and in changed cultural contexts, while still maintaining the integrity and objectivity of the revelation which those doctrines, rituals and institutions exist to articulate. The *Essay on Development* has remained the essential touchstone for all subsequent explorations of the issues it first identified: idiosyncratic, incomplete and tentative as it is, it is a landmark in Christian thought worthy of mention alongside more systematic classics like Augustine's *City of God*, Aquinas' *Summa* or Calvin's *Institutes*.

3
Faith and doubt

Newman's philosophical outlook was formed in the empiricist tradition that stemmed from John Locke. In that tradition, sound religious faith was the product of a rational assessment of the evidence for beliefs such as God's existence or the inerrancy of the Bible: as Archbishop John Tillotson wrote '... all assent must be *grounded upon evidence*; that is, no man can believe any thing, unless he have, or think he hath, some reason to do so. For to be confident of a thing without reason is not faith, but a presumptuous persuasion and obstinacy of mind.'[52] The young Newman's philosophical mentor at Oriel, Richard Whately, agreed: Christian faith was distinguished from superstition by 'its resting on evidence; – by its offering a reason, – and requiring Christians to be able to give a reason, for believing it.'[53] Accordingly, works like William Paley's *Natural Theology: Evidences of the being and Attributes of the Deity* mustered 'proofs' for the truth of Christianity, drawn largely from the physical sciences, and became a staple of early nineteenth century university instruction.[54]

The Romantic Movement, of which Newman was a product, rejected all this: how could faith in the living God be the outcome of a cold bean-counting calculation, an exercise of mere mind, and not a movement of the longing heart? As Samuel Taylor Coleridge wrote, 'Evidences of Christianity! I am weary of the word. Make a man feel the want of it; rouse him, if you can, to the self-knowledge of his need of it; and you may safely trust it to its own Evidence ...'[55] Newman shared that perception, and in the *Oxford University Sermons* he preached in the late 1830s, explored its implications for a right understanding of the relationship between faith and reason. The eighteenth century, he thought, had been 'a time when love was cold', and so had been 'especially the age of evidences'. Though not entirely discounting their value, he was acutely aware of the vulnerability of 'proofs' of the existence of God drawn from the natural world: 'It is a great question whether Atheism is not as philosophically consistent with the phenomena of the physical world ... as the doctrine of a creative and governing Power.'[56] Man, he insisted elsewhere, 'is not a reasoning animal; he is a seeing, feeling, contemplating, acting animal ...' and therefore 'The heart is commonly reached, not through the reason, but through the imagination, by means of direct impressions, by the testimony of facts and events, by history, by description. Persons influence us, voices melt us, looks subdue us, deeds inflame us. Many a man will live and die upon a dogma: no man will be a martyr for a conclusion.'[57]

Newman was not here justifying irrationality, the triumph of heart over head: instead, he was proposing a different model of what human reason actually was. Instead of the simplistic Enlightenment image of rationality as a neutral weighing up of evidence until the balance tipped in favour of a conclusion, he pointed to the complex ways in which human beings actually arrive at their core convictions, in science and daily life just as much as in religion.

> The mind ranges to and fro, and spreads out, and advances forward with a quickness which has become a proverb, and a subtlety and versatility which baffle investigation. It passes on from point to point, gaining one by some indication; another on a probability; then availing itself of an association; then falling back on some received law; next seizing on testimony; then committing itself to some popular impression, or some inward instinct, or some obscure memory; and thus it makes progress not unlike a clamberer on a steep cliff, who, by quick eye, prompt hand, and firm foot, ascends how he knows not himself; by personal endowments and by practice, rather than by rule, leaving no track behind him, and unable to teach another. … And such mainly is the way in which all men, gifted or not gifted, commonly reason – not by rule, but by an inward faculty.[58]

That 'inner faculty' he called 'Implicit reason', 'a living, spontaneous energy within us, not an art', as distinct from Explicit reason, the 'reflective power of the human mind, contemplating and scrutinizing its own acts'. It was a fatal error to confuse these two quite separate exercises, and to privilege the secondary business of analyzing our thinking over the primary and often intuitive processes by which everyone except logicians arrive at the conclusions that guide action. Human beings on the whole 'do not reason incorrectly: they may argue badly but they reason well'. In other words, 'all men have a reason, but not all men can give a reason.'[59]

Newman pushed his critique of Enlightenment models of the grounds for religious certainty further, by challenging the idea that right thought is essentially neutral. It was a mistake to imagine that in searching for truth 'there is no room for choice; there is no merit, no praise or blame, in believing or disbelieving ... that a man is as little responsible for his faith as for his bodily functions.' On the contrary, 'a man is responsible for his faith, because he is responsible for his likings and dislikings, his hopes and opinions, on all of which his faith depends.' In the process of arriving at our moral or political or religious choices, nobody starts with a blank sheet: what we find plausible or persuasive, what we take to be true, will be influenced by 'antecedent probabilities' – the network of prior beliefs and assumptions, past experiences, moral habits and temperamental inclinations which shape our judgements: the Enlightenment insistence that the rational man is an unbiased calculator had no basis in human nature as it really is. That was why arguments that seem strong and persuasive to one person, fail to move another. Our moral and religious conclusions reflect the kind of person our deliberate choices have made us, and so faith 'is the reasoning of a religious mind, or of what Scripture calls a right or renewed heart, which acts on presumptions rather than evidence.' We are disposed to believe in what we have learned to love or hope for, and 'it is almost a proverb, that persons believe what they wish to be true.'[60]

Newman of course recognized the dangers of 'wishful thinking': the 'antecedent probabilities' that lead us towards particular conclusions 'may be equally available for what is true, and what pretends to be true'. But he considered that the best protection against 'credulity and superstition' was not a hermeneutic of suspicion, resolving to doubt everything except what could be proved from hard 'evidence', but 'a right state of the heart'. It was a fatal error for the worldly to imagine themselves judges of religious truth, 'without preparation of heart'. Mountains of dead evidence could produce nothing but a dead faith, whereas a heart rightly disposed can discern in even imperfect and partial hints and glimpses the reality of

God: 'a mutilated and defective evidence suffices for persuasion where the heart is alive'. In all the important actions of life, the 'venture of faith' was a necessity of human nature:

> We are so constituted, that if we insist upon being as sure as is conceivable, in every step of our course, we must be content to creep along the ground, and can never soar. If we are intended for great ends, we are called to great hazards; and, whereas we are given absolute certainty in nothing, we must in all things choose between doubt and inactivity ...[61]

For Newman that right disposition of the heart was above all rooted in obedience to conscience. Within every human breast, pagan or Christian, educated or uneducated, there was a faculty which by its very existence provided an inescapable witness to the reality of a higher power, 'not a mere opinion, or impression, or view of things, but a law, an authoritative voice, bidding him do certain things and avoid others.' Though the voice of conscience in any given individual might be obscured, inconsistent, even mistaken when distorted by sin or error, nevertheless, the very existence of conscience, and the fact that it 'commands, it praises, it blames, it promises, it threatens, it implies a future, and it witnesses the unseen', all this 'throws us out of ourselves, and beyond ourselves, to go and seek Him in the height and the depth, whose Voice it is'.[62] This insistence that the most importance single witness to the reality of God was the voice of conscience within every human being was one of Newman's most characteristic and consistent teachings: in his controversy with Gladstone over infallibility, Newman would go so far as the call conscience '"the aboriginal Vicar of Christ'. It is also one of the most controversial of his ideas, not least because in its most carefully articulated form, in the *Grammar of Assent*, he gave to it an emotional colouring that, as Sir Anthony Kenny has observed, cannot be read by a post-Freudian generation 'without acute discomfort'. Newman wrote that

> If, on doing wrong, we feel the same tearful, broken hearted sorrow which overwhelms us on hurting a mother; if, on doing right, we enjoy the same sunny serenity of mind, the same soothing satisfactory delight which follows on our receiving praise from a father, we certainly have within us the image of some person, to whom our love and veneration look, in whose smile we find our happiness, for whom we yearn, towards whom we direct our pleadings, in whose anger we are troubled and waste away. These feelings in us are such as require for their exciting cause an intelligent being.[63]

Newman's preoccupation with the rationality of belief was heightened in the 1860s by his friendship with the distinguished naval engineer, William Froude, younger brother of his closest Oxford friend, Richard Hurrell Froude. Froude's wife and all but one of his children became Catholics under Newman's influence. Yet Froude himself remained a sceptic, convinced that scientific reasoning was the only legitimate model for all enquiries after truth, and therefore that all 'certainties' whatever were purely provisional, exactly proportional to the hard evidence that could be adduced for them. Their extended and fascinating correspondence lay behind Newman's most technical philosophical work, endlessly drafted and redrafted over the course of many years, and published in 1870 as *The Grammar of Assent*. In the *Grammar* Newman refined, systematized and extended the ideas which had been set out in the *Oxford University Sermons* and the letters on the *Tamworth Reading Room*. The idea of 'Implicit Reasoning' was now given the name 'the Illative sense', an informal but generally reliable faculty of discernment that underlay all our assents, which Newman likened to Aristotle's idea of *Phronesis*, wisdom or practical intelligence, and which he compared to aesthetic judgement or taste, which may be good or bad, which is generally considered to be objective, yet about whose judgements argument was often difficult to resolve. The demand of thinkers like Froude for perfectly objective standards of proof was the pursuit of an illusion, the attempt to force human intelligence into forms alien to it.

> I am what I am, or I am nothing. I cannot think, reflect, or judge about my being, without starting from the very point which I aim at concluding. My ideas are all assumptions, and I am ever moving in a circle. I cannot avoid being sufficient for myself, for I cannot make myself anything else, and to change me is to destroy me. If I do not use myself, I have no other self to use. My only business is to ascertain what I am, in order to put it to use. It is enough for the proof of the value and authority of any function which I possess, to be able to pronounce that it is natural. What I have to ascertain is the laws under which I live. My first elementary lesson of duty is that of resignation to the laws of my nature, whatever they are; my first disobedience is to be impatient at what I am, and to indulge an ambitious aspiration after what I cannot be, to cherish a distrust of my powers, and to desire to change laws which are identical with myself.[64]

This was no mere concession to religion, an attempt to justify faith on weak and insufficient grounds. All our important certainties were acquired by a similar exercise of judgement.

> in no class of concrete reasonings, whether in experimental science, historical research, or theology, is there any ultimate test of truth and error in our inferences besides the trustworthiness of the Illative Sense that gives them its sanction; just as there is no sufficient test of poetical excellence, heroic action, or gentleman-like conduct, other than the particular mental sense, be it genius, taste, sense of propriety, or the moral sense, to which those subject-matters are severally committed. Our duty in each of these is to strengthen and perfect the special faculty which is its living rule, and in every case as it comes to do our best.[65]

Much of the *Grammar* was devoted to arguing that there were no degrees in assent: we either believe something to be true, or we do not. This was part of Newman's wider rejection of the Lockean notion that any particular belief could only be as strong as the solid weight of the evidence for it. Yet it was fundamental to Newman's analysis that in point of fact we often come to firmly held convictions – certitudes – on the basis of intuitions or fragments of evidence which suggest to us greater patterns. He had deeply internalized the teaching of the eighteenth century Bishop of Durham, Joseph Butler, that 'Probability is the guide of life'. Rationalists of Froude's kind rejected that model of thinking on the grounds that ten weak arguments do not add up to one good one. Newman challenged that assumption. As he explained to a correspondent in 1864:

> The best illustration of what I hold is that of a cable which is made up of a number of separate threads, each feeble, yet together as sufficient as an iron rod. An iron rod represents mathematical or strict demonstration; a cable represents moral demonstration, which is an assemblage of

> probabilities, separately insufficient for certainty, but, when put together, irrefragable. A man who said 'I cannot trust a cable, I must have an iron bar,' would, in certain given cases, be irrational and unreasonable: so too is a man who says I must have a rigid demonstration, not moral demonstration, of religious truth.[66]

Until fairly recently, Newman's writings on the nature of belief were very largely ignored by mainstream philosophers, probably because of his explicitly (and unfashionably) religious agenda. More recently, however, the range, sophistication and originality of his account of the phenomenology of belief are coming to be recognized. In his last letter to William Froude, Newman wrote:

> We differ in our sense and use of the word 'certain'. I use it of minds, you of propositions. I fully grant the uncertainty of all conclusions in your sense of the word, but I maintain that minds may in my sense be certain of conclusions which are uncertain in yours.[67]

Newman is sometimes criticized for slipping illegitimately from a powerful and subtle analysis of how in fact we acquire our certitutudes, to suggesting that what we believe with certitude is likely to be true: the criticism has some force, though he was clear that even our certitudes might be mistaken. His argument that conscience is the most powerful single evidence for the existence of a personal God is vulnerable to counter-claims that there are perfectly satisfactory naturalistic explanations for the universal possession of a moral faculty. Yet the argument from conscience has been taken up and developed by distinguished modern philosophers of religion like Alvin Plantinga, and the *University Sermons* and, especially, the *Grammar of Assent*, anticipate many of the concerns, strategies and conclusions of the later Wittgenstein in *On Certainty*.[68] At the very least in the subtlety and range of its analysis of the processes by which we attain our certainties the *Grammar* is a major contribution to the psychology of belief. In philosophy, as in theology, Newman remains a force to be reckoned with.

4
Newman's Catholicism

The Catholic Church Newman joined in October 1845 was increasingly centred round the Pope. The collapse after the French Revolution of many the authoritarian regimes that had prevailed under the *Ancien Regime* stripped the church of its age-old monopoly over education and religious formation, and left it at odds with increasingly hostile or indifferent secular societies. In a world bereft of its ancient landmarks, papal authority seemed to offer a rock round which counter-cultural resistance could rally. Gregory XVI, pope when Newman moved from Anglicanism to Catholicism, carried his loathing of modernity so far as to exclude the railways from the papal states. His successor, Pio Nono, was at first less confrontational (and an enthusiast for the railway), but his superficial 'liberalism' evaporated after the revolutions of 1848, when he himself fled Rome for sanctuary in Neopolitan territory. Papa Pio's confrontation with the modern world would intensify as the movement for Italian unification eroded and eventually abolished the Papal States, the thousand-year old basis of the papacy's political autonomy – and finances.

Newman the convert naturally shared this ardent reverence for the papacy, and his publications of the 1850s credited the Holy See 'over and above the attribute of infallibility' with 'a gift of sagacity, [that] had in every age characterized its occupants', even on purely practical matters.[69] But in private his enthusiasm became increasingly qualified. Newman believed the Church to be infallible, but located infallibility in the whole community, represented primarily by the Pope in Council, and only secondarily in the Pope alone – he told an Anglican correspondent in 1851 that 'I must protest with all my might against what I consider an assumption, that the infallibility of the Pope is the basis of the Catholic Religion... . There are persons who have found Papal Infallibility to be the gate; let them, if they will – our minds are so differently constituted that proof and difficulty change places in the case of separate persons.'[70] Increasingly repelled by the extreme papalism of 'ultramontane' former friends and disciples like W. G. Ward, Henry Edward Manning, and Fr Faber's troublesome community at the Brompton Oratory, Newman came to a more sober assessment of the central authorities in papal Rome. July 1859 was a milestone in this shift, when he published a controversial article in the liberal Catholic magazine, whose editorship he had reluctantly accepted, *The Rambler*. 'On consulting the faithful in matters of doctrine' drew on Newman's patristic researches to argue that during the Arian crisis most of the episcopate had fallen into error, and whole provinces of the Church led by their bishops had succumbed to the Arian or semi-arian heresies. Popes, patriarchs and even General Councils 'had said what they should not have said', and instead the laity had become the defenders of the faith: 'the divine dogma of our Lord's divinity was proclaimed, enforced, maintained and (humanly speaking) preserved far more by the "Ecclesia docta" than by the "Ecclesia docens".' In terms familiar from his *Anglican Lectures on the Prophetical Office*, he argued that Apostolic tradition expresses itself at various times through different means – sometimes through the hierarchy, sometimes through theologians, sometimes through the people, sometimes through liturgy or through customs or movements thrown up by particular historical moments. Consequently 'the body of the faithful is one of the witnesses to the fact of the tradition of revealed doctrine, and … their consensus through Christendom is the voice of the Infallible church.'[71] The suggestion that the hierarchy might lead the faithful into heresy, and that the laity, not the clergy, might on occasion be God's instruments in preserving the true faith was anathema in the age of Pio Nono, where a sharp distinction between the (clerical) teaching Church and the (largely lay) *taught* Church was taken for granted. Newman was delated to Rome as a heretic: demands for explanations were misunderstood or not passed on to him, and his failure to explain was interpreted as defiance.

He failed to satisfy Rome on other accounts also. Since 1859 the forces of Italian unification had stripped Pio Nono of most of the papal patrimony which had once stretched from Tuscany to Naples, leaving him master only of the city of Rome and part of Latzio. The world was treated to the unedifying spectacle of a Pope holding the people of his remaining territories subject with the aid of a foreign army. Nevertheless, in a Europe most of whose peoples were Catholics, most, including, to begin with, Newman, considered that the Father of all the faithful should not be the subject of a particular nation, but should have his own political sovereignty. Ultramontanes like Manning, Cardinal Wiseman's right-hand man and eventual successor, gave all this a theological rationale. The Pope's political authority, Manning argued, was the cornerstone of a world order rooted in the Incarnation. The Papacy's historic role as arbiter of international law, anointing and deposing kings, embodied the rule of Christ in the world he had redeemed, without which political society was reduced to mere brute power, the triumph of the weak over the strong. The temporal sovereignty of the Pope was therefore 'the key-stone of the arch' of Christian civilization. Cavour and Garibaldi's attempts to annexe the Papal States for Italy were part of an age-old struggle between God and antiChrist. The city of Rome 'is the only spot of ground on which the Vicar of Christ can set the sole of his foot in freedom' and therefore 'they who would drive the Incarnation off the face of the earth hover about it to wrest it from his hands.'[72]

Unsurprisingly, many people wondered what the best mind in the Catholic Church thought about all this. In his stridently polemical 1850 lectures on the *Difficulties of Anglicans*, Newman himself had deployed the familiar trope of the providential protection of Papal Rome, recalling that however often Pope had been exiled from their city, always when the mists and upheavals of revolution cleared, 'the old man is found in his own place, as before, saying Mass over the tomb of the Apostles.'[73] Yet Newman privately agreed with the widespread Protestant view that the Papal States were in fact badly governed. In anonymous contributions to the letter pages of the *Rambler* in 1859 he commented on 'the slovenly, disgraceful way in which things go on' in Italy, where, though 'religion is not indeed extinct' it 'seems to me to be in a state of spiritual decadence', a situation he blamed on poor government – by implication poor papal government.[74]

Newman's views were increasingly shaped by dismay at the calamitous stand-off he perceived between educated Italian lay opinion on one hand, and an increasingly intransigent clericalist ultramontanism on the other, whose wholesale repudiation of modernity was forcing Italian intellect 'to grow wild: in consequence it rebels'. Papal Catholicism in Italy, he thought, relied on repression and authority, when what was needed was conversion, education, persuasion.[75] In 1866, forced by Garibaldi's march on Rome to take a public stand on the Temporal Power, Newman preached a sermon on the subject which was a masterpiece of careful casuistry, the unenthusiastic sound of one hand clapping.[76] In it, he dutifully described the Pope's Italian enemies as 'sacrilegious robbers'. But he also acknowledged political realities: 'While his subjects are for him, no one can have a word to say against his temporal rule; but who can force a Sovereign on a people which deliberately rejects him?' He had often deplored in private the hysterical rhetoric of Ultramontanes 'almost giving up the Church, if the temporal power went, shrieking as if [they] were on the edge of an abyss.'[77] Now he publicly poured cold water on any idea that the temporal Power was essential to the work of the Church. If the Pope lost the Papal States, he merely 'returns to the condition of St Sylvester, St Julius, St Innocent, and other great Popes of early times.' If God's providence removed the Temporal Power, it would be because it was no longer necessary for the Church's mission.

Newman committed himself on the Temporal Power with extreme reluctance: it was, he considered, a matter of politics and so 'out of my way'. But he was also intensely conscious that it had become a test issue for an ultraCatolicism intent on narrowing and tightening the bounds of orthodoxy, under the cloak of loyalty to a suffering pope, and keen to unchurch anyone who dissented. In 1867 he told James Hope Scott,

> ...there is a great attempt ... to bring in a new theory of Papal Infallibility, which would make it a mortal sin ... not to hold the Temporal Power necessary to the Papacy. No one

> answers them, and multitudes are being carried away – the Pope … gives ear to them, and the consequence is there is a very extreme prejudice in the highest quarters at Rome against such as me.[78]

Behind all this lay a lack of confidence in God's providence, a tyranny of fear. He told Emily Bowles, to whom he always wrote frankly,

> we are shrinking into ourselves, narrowing the lines of communion, trembling at freedom of thought, and using the language of dismay and despair at the prospect before us …[79]

As a Catholic, Newman had always carefully refused the title 'theologian', a word he identified with technical expertise in the minutiae of official Church teaching. He told his old friend Maria Giberne in February 1869:

> really and truly I am <u>not</u> a theologian. A theologian is one who has mastered theology – who can say how many opinions there are on every point, what authors have taken which, and which is best – who can discriminate exactly between proposition and proposition, argument and argument, who can pronounce which are safe, which allowable, which dangerous – who can trace the history of doctrines in successive centuries, and apply the principles of former times to the conditions of the present. This it is to be a theologian – this and a hundred things besides. And this I am not and never shall be … .[80]

In the so called 'Munich Brief' of 1863, Pope Pius IX attacked the European Liberal Catholic movement headed by Henry

Lacordaire and the Count Montalambert, insisting that Catholic scholars were bound

> not only by the solemn definitions of the Church, but also by the ordinary magisterium, the decisions of the Roman Curial Congregations, and by the common teaching of the theologians.[81]

So Newman understood that theology was conceived by the Roman authorities as a form of licensed commentary on official (hierarchical) teaching, as lawyers might interpret the Law Reports. Although he never publicly challenged this unernourished understanding of theology, he repeatedly deplored the lack of debate within the Church, and the suffocating effects of the uniformity expected at Rome. So his careful deference to the expertise of the Roman theologians, though not entirely strategic, had very strict limits.[82] He was intensely conscious of the ignorance of the writings of the Fathers among even the most learned Roman theologians, so although, as he was to tell the Duke of Norfolk many years later, while at Rome 'the rules of interpreting authoritative documents are known with a perfection which at this time is scarcely to be found elsewhere', nevertheless he privately considered that a really first-rate theologian was rarely to be found there.[83]

Newman certainly *did* consider himself a theologian in this broader and more original sense. He had hoped after becoming a Catholic that he and his colleagues in what eventually became the Oratory might found a distinctively English *Schola Theologorum*, which would bend its energies to encountering the unbelief of the age.[84] He abandoned that idea, but he certainly continued to think of the work he did as theological. The bitter experience of the hostile response to his essay *On Consulting the Faithful*, however, was to bring home to him the difficulty of doing theology at all in the church of Pio Nono. In 1863 he told Emily Bowles,

> to write theology is like dancing on the tight-rope some hundred feet above ground: it is hard to keep from falling, and the fall is great.[85]

Newman, in fact, came to believe that the calamity of modern Catholicism was precisely the absence of free theological debate. In 1875 at the height of his exasperation with the ultramontanes, he wrote,

> [Manning] is not a theologian, the Pope is not a theologian, and therefore theology has gone out of fashion … . I don't profess to be a theologian, but at all events I should have been able to show a side of the Catholic religion more theological, more exact, than [theirs].[86]

For him, as we shall see, theology was not the docile interpreter of the magisterium, but the 'regulating principle' of the Church, without which authority inevitably exceeded its bounds and distorted Christian truth. Dogmatic utterances were one thing, and were for him a given, but their *meaning* could only be elicited by theological debate, without which they remained a lifeless skeleton or an intellectual straitjacket. And he conceived theological enquiry and debate not as the search for immediate consensus under the guidance of authority, but as genuinely open-ended, and often conflictual, a process in which personal struggle, insight and genius, not institutional docility, led to breakthrough. In discussing the role of theology he consistently deployed the rhetoric of conflict, tension and strain. It could not be otherwise, he wrote in an exuberant passage of the *Apologia*, his metaphors clearly influenced by his ministry in a great industrial city, since the universal church was 'a vast assemblage of human beings with wilful intellects and wild passions, brought together … into what may be called a large reformatory or training-school', not a hospital or a prison, and emphatically not 'in order to be sent to bed, not to be buried alive', but 'for the melting, refining, and moulding, as in some moral factory, by an incessant noisy process, of the raw material of human nature, so excellent, so dangerous, so capable of divine purposes.'[87]

In former times, he wrote in 1872, 'it was by the *collision* of Catholic intellects with Catholic intellects that the meaning and limit of dogmatic decrees were determined', but in the contemporary church 'there has been no intellectual scrutiny, no controversies'.[88] Even before the Council, he complained that anyone attempting original theological work was like a slave working 'under the lash', and he told Emily Bowles

> This age of the Church is peculiar. In former times there was not the extreme centralisation which is now in use. If a private theologian said anything, another answered him. If the controversy grew, then it went to a Bishop, a theological Faculty, or to some foreign university. The Holy See was but the court of ultimate appeal. Now, if I as a private priest put anything in print, Propaganda answers me at once. How can I fight with such a chain on my arm? ... There was true private judgement in the primitive and medieval schools. There are no schools now, no private judgement (in the religious sense of the phrase) no freedom of opinion. That is, no exercise of the intellect. This is a way of things which in God's own time, will work its own cure of necessity".[89]

Unsurprisingly, Newman took a low view of some of the most celebrated papal utterances of his own day: he thought that the 1864 encyclical *Quanta cura* and especially its accompanying 'Syllabus of Errors', designed as a blast against 'liberal' ideas in church and state, was a theological mess, made up of scattergun denunciations of matters in which the Church had no real expertise and over which it had no legitimate jurisdiction, its terminology too sloppy to carry any real authority even with Catholics. 'There seems nothing … in it', he thought, 'which looks like a theological decision' and, 'if it is urged against me as such, I should [be] obliged to fall back upon my liberty in opinion, till that liberty is proved to be taken away.' Yet he was not altogether sorry that the *Syllabus* had been issued: it had highlighted the limits of authority in the Church and, as he told a correspondent in 1865,

> Everything is good which brings matters to a crisis. It is not the matter of the document, but the animus of its authors, and their mode of doing it, which is so trying. Will not the next century demand Popes who are not Italians?[90]

The warm reception of the *Apologia* emboldened Newman to make his views known, and from 1865 he went on the offensive against the extremism which he felt was distorting perception of the Church, both within and without her boundaries. With the prospect of a General Council looming, Pusey published in 1865 an open letter to Keble, ostensibly an 'Eirenicon' designed to open the way to the reunion of the Roman Catholic and Anglican Churches, but containing an extended attack on papal infallibility and the extravagances of Catholic Mariology – as Newman commented ironically to his old friend, 'You discharge your olive-branch as if from a catapult'. Manning and the late Father Faber featured prominently among the authorities Pusey cited, including Faber's bizarre claim that the flesh of Mary was received along with that of Jesus in the Eucharist.[91]

Newman seized the opportunity to appear as a champion of Catholic truth, and in the process to dissociate himself publicly from the ultramontanes. Studiously deferential to Manning, now Archbishop of Westminster, and lyrically laudatory about Faber, whom in life he had come to detest, he nevertheless made no bones about his rejection of their views: they were 'in no sense spokesmen for English Catholics':

> I prefer English habits of belief and devotion to foreign … In following those of my people, I show less singularity, and create less disturbance than if I made a flourish with what is novel and exotic.[92]

He could not allow Pusey, he insisted,

> to identify the doctrine of our Oxford friends in question … with the present spirit or the prospective creed of Catholics; or to assume, as you do, that, because they are thorough-going and relentless in their statements, therefore they are the harbingers of a new age when to show a deference to Antiquity will be thought little else than a mistake.

Newman's own Catholic faith had been arrived at through the study of the Fathers, and everything a Catholic needed to believe would be found in them, though sometimes in a developed form.

> The Fathers made me a Catholic, and I am not going to kick down the ladder by which I ascended into the Church. It is

> a ladder quite as serviceable for that purpose now, as it was twenty years ago.[93]

The *Letter to Pusey* confirmed Manning's opposition to all Newman stood for: as he told the Pope's close adviser, Mgr George Talbot, Newman was 'the centre of those who hold low views about the Holy See, are anti-Roman … national, critical of Catholic devotions, and always on the lower side.' Newman embodied the 'highest type' of 'the old Anglican patristic, literary tone transplanted into the Church …. In one word, it is worldly Catholicism.' Talbot concurred: to be truly Roman he thought, required an effort for any Englishman, and Newman was 'more English than the English – His spirit must be crushed.'[94]

Newman declined a papal invitation to attend the Vatican Council as a theological consultant. He pleaded age, ill-health and other pressing work, but his refusal reflected his strong opposition to the campaign for the definition of papal infallibility, not because he rejected the doctrine, rightly understood, but because he believed that in the church of Pio Nono, with its lop-sided insistence on centralized authority, it was almost impossible that the doctrine should be rightly understood. In a private jotting in September 1869 he asked, 'Why is it, if I believe the Pope's Infallibility I do not wish it defined? is not truth a gain? I answer, because it can't be so defined as not to raise more questions than it solves … "Woe unto those thro' whom scandals come".'[95] The definition was not needed – there was no heresy within the church questioning Papal authority. To define infallibility would unbalance 'the elementary Constitution of the Church' by encouraging the Pope to act without consultation with other bishops, and it would stir up fruitless controversies about past papal teaching.[96] In the notorious leaked letter to his bishop in January 1870, he denounced the campaign for the definition as the work of an 'insolent aggressive faction', a 'clique of Jesuits, Redemptorists and converts', imposing unnecessary burdens on the consciences of the faithful: the pope himself was to blame for encouraging that faction.

> What have we done to be treated, as the faithful never were treated before? When has definition of doctrine de fide been a luxury of devotion, and not a stern painful necessity?[97]

Late in 1870 he wrote bitterly,

> We have come to a climax of tyranny. It is not good for a Pope to live 20 years. It is an anomaly and bears no good fruit; he becomes a god, has no one to contradict him, does not know facts, and does cruel things without meaning it.[98]

Though he eventually accepted the definition, and counselled others to do so, he believed it needed and would ultimately receive correction. As he wrote in 1871:

> The late definition does not so much need to be undone, as to be completed. It needs safeguards to the Pope's possible acts – explanations as to the matter and extent of his power. I know that a violent reckless party, had it its will, would at this moment define that the Pope's powers need no safeguards, no explanations – but there is a limit to the triumph of the tyrannical – Let us be patient, let us have faith, and a new Pope, and a re-assembled Council may trim the boat."[99]

In fact, in the light of the definition, Newman came to think that the end of the papal temporal power might even be a necessary part of that 'trimming of the boat'. Already in 1866 he had agreed with his friend Bishop Moriarty of Kerry that if a secular government took power in Rome, it would be very likely to impose censorship on the correspondence of the Curial Congregations. But, he had added, this might not be altogether a bad thing:

> there is no evil without its alleviation – it would cut off a great deal of unprofitable gossip sent to Rome from the *orbis terrarum*, and of crude answers sent back from Rome by men who seem to have authority, but have none – and it would throw power into the hands of the local Bishops every where.[100]

By the end of 1870, he was even wondering whether the annexation of Rome by the new Italy might not in fact be a divine judgement on the conduct of the Council. It would surely be a providential restraint on the future abuse of papal power: as he told his friend Mrs William Froude,

> … to be at once infallible in religion and a despot in temporals, is perhaps too great for mortal man … unless the Council, when re-assembled, qualifies the dogma by some considerable safeguards … perhaps the secularly defenceless state of the Pope will oblige him to court that Catholic body in its separate nations with a considerateness and kindness, which of late years the Holy See has not shown, and which may effectually prevent a tyrannous use of his spiritual power. But all these things are in God's hands, and we are blind.[101]

Ironically, in 1874 Newman was to publish what remains a classic defence of the doctrine of papal infallibility, his

Letter to the Duke of Norfolk. But that pamphlet represented not a conversion to enthusiasm for what had happened at the Council, but a damage-limitation exercise, designed to emphasize the narrow extent of what had been defined, and to show that the definition of Infallibility had no implications for whether or not Catholics could be good citizens of a non-Catholic state. It was one of Newman's most courageous utterances, for, four years on from the adjournment of the Council, he reminded his readers that he had been strongly opposed to the definition, reaffirmed the contents of the leaked letter to Ullathorne, once more deploring the campaign for the definition: 'I felt deeply and ever shall feel … the violence and cruelty of those who by their reckless and rash language had employed themselves in "unsettling the weak in faith, throwing back enquirers, and shocking the Protestant mind".' He set out some of the factors that had led him to accept the definition, in the process emphasizing the very concept which had got him into bad odour at Rome in 1859, namely, the role of the *sensus fidelium*. A strong motive for assent would be if 'the definition is consistently received by the whole body of the faithful, as valid, or as expression of a truth … by the force of that great dictum, "Securus judicat orbis terrarum".'[102] He explained that the definition was an example of the development of doctrine, and then went on to offer a carefully minimalist reading of what had actually been defined. Definition was one thing: interpreting what the definition implied was another, for, when the Church defines a dogma, she 'sets her theologians to work to explain her meaning in the concrete'. Claiming that prerogative, Newman cited Roman theologians like Peronne to emphasize that infallibility was a negative gift, not a habit of mind or any kind of inspiration: it was an external aid to prevent the pope – and the Church – from going astray in solemn definitions of doctrine, bearing directly on faith or morals. Such definitions were and should be, he insisted, very rare indeed: on other matters, the pope's private opinions were – opinions – though to be treated with profound respect as coming from him. In moral matters the Pope was bound by natural law, so cannot command anything sinful, just as the faithful were bound by their consciences. In the almost impossible event of a real clash between conscience and pope, a Catholic would sin if they disregarded conscience and obeyed the Pope, an insistence Newman emphasized in the celebrated and consciously provocative toast 'to Conscience first, and to the Pope afterwards.'[103]

That toast has often been misunderstood, as if Newman was suggesting a stark opposition between conscience and ecclesiastical authority. But his teaching on the subject was more complex. On the one hand, was an exalted view of the authority of conscience as 'the aboriginal Vicar of Christ, a prophet in its informations, a monarch in its peremptoriness, a priest in its blessings and anathemas, and, even though the eternal priesthood throughout the Church could cease to be, in it the sacerdotal principle would remain and would have a sway.' On the other hand, our sense of right and wrong 'is so delicate, so fitful, so easily puzzled, obscured, perverted' by education, pride or passion, that conscience is at once 'the highest of all teachers, yet the least luminous.' It is the heart of natural religion, but natural religion needs to be 'sustained and completed by revelation'. Church, pope and hierarchy therefore supply the guidance that the natural limitations of conscience 'urgently demand'.[104]

Yet the *Letter* was also daring in including a masterly deconstruction of the authority and significance of overweening magisterium in the shape of the *Syllabus of Errors*, issued in 1864, which Newman dismisses as a mere anonymous list of errors with no direct authorization by the Pope, so that 'I do not see my way to accept it for what it is not'.[105] The *Syllabus* 'has no dogmatic force' and 'cannot even be called an echo of the Apostolic Voice'. And he levelled a contemptuous aside at those around the Pope, egging him on to excesses: the 'Rock of St Peter on its summit enjoys a pure and serene atmosphere, but there is a great deal of Roman malaria at the foot of it.'[106] By implication, the *Syllabus* was a manifestation of that 'malaria'. The Pope's 'great earnestness and charity' were being sabotaged by 'circles of light-minded men in his city' who, Newman claimed, had been 'laying bets with each other whether the Syllabus would "make a row in Europe"'.[107]

It was in the light of his continuing concern with the scope of the Infallibility decree that in 1877 Newman would publish what some consider his theological masterpiece, a short preface to a new edition of his Anglican lectures on the Prophetical Office. In this preface he argued that there was and always should be a healthy tension in the life of the Church between authority, theological exploration and the spiritual and sacramental aspects of the Church: these three different and contrasting energies were perpetually engaged in a dance of mutual correction and complementarity, which could not without peril be resolved by the permanent subordination of any one to the others. His discussion starts from an objection often raised against the Catholic Church, not least by his younger Protestant self, namely the 'discordance' between the claims to purity of Catholic theology on the one hand, and the apparent superstition of much Catholic devotional practice and the corruption of 'ecclesiastics in high positions', on the other. But his real target audience was undoubtedly those within the Church, from the Pope downwards, whose actions and ideas he believed were distorting contemporary Catholicism, and damaging the Church's credibility in evangelising an unbelieving world.

For Newman, as we have seen, it was by what he called 'the collision of Catholic intellect with Catholic intellect' that in times past 'the meaning and limits of dogmatic decrees were determined.'[108] Debate and disagreement were essential to the Church's apprehension of the truths she preached: 'Truth is wrought out by many minds, working together freely. As far as I can make out, this has ever been the rule of the Church till now.'[109] But, as he remarked to Frederick Rogers, his favourite Oxford pupil, the Catholic Church's mission to modern society was hamstrung by a morbid fear of theological novelty, so that theologians 'cannot move in matters of speculation … without giving enormous scandal to our people … I have long wished to write an Essay, but I never shall, I think, on the conflicting interests, and therefore difficulties of the Catholic Church, because she is at once, first, a devotion, secondly a philosophy, thirdly a polity. Just now, as I suppose at many other times the devotional sentiment and the political *embarrass* the philosophical instinct.'[110]

Newman's argument in the *Preface* therefore replaced a monolithic understanding of the Church, in which hierarchy or governance determine all aspects of religious life, with a far more dynamic model, in which three divergent but complementary energies, principles or 'offices' exist in permanent creative tension. Newman had deployed triadic models of ecclesial life in earlier writings: here he relates these threefold energies to the threefold offices which are united in Christ – the prophetic, standing variously for revelation, teaching, theology, rational thought: the priestly, representing the spiritual, devotional, or what Friedrich von Hugel would later call the *mystical* element of religion: and the kingly or royal office, representing rule, governance, structure, institution, which he here identifies with the Pope and the Curia. In Nicholas Lash's lapidary summary, Christianity is 'at one and the same time life in the spirit, language, and organization.'[111]

These three powers or offices were all vital constituents of the concrete historical reality of the Body of Christ. But their different objects and scope inevitably pull them in different directions:

> Truth is the guiding principle of theology and theological inquiries; devotion and edification, of worship; and of government, expedience. The instrument of theology is reasoning: of worship, our emotional nature; of rule, command and coercion. Further, in man as he is, reasoning tends to rationalism, devotion to superstition and enthusiasm; and power to ambition and tyranny.[112]

So the balance between the three is always precarious, and in practice never adequately attained:

> Who, even with divine aid, shall successfully administer offices so independent of each other, so divergent and so conflicting? What line of conduct, except on the long, the very long run, is at once edifying, expedient, and true?[113]

The bulk of the preface is taken up with concrete historical examples of the ways in which this unceasing interplay between these three offices has worked out, such as Pope Stephen's ruling that Donatist baptisms were valid, a piece of pastoral expediency in which a pope overruled the best theological opinion of the day, but which turned out to be a wise and necessary concession to the demands of unity and charity.

Newman's argument is not always clear: what, precisely, is the relationship in his analysis between revelation and theology? The *Preface* is constrained and at times impoverished by Newman's sometimes uncritical deployment of nineteenth century theological categories, for example in his apparent reduction of the sacral dimension of Christianity to religious emotion or even popular superstition. There is no suggestion in the *Preface* of the fundamentally sacramental nature of the Church or the centrality of the liturgy to its very being, though both those themes recur frequently elsewhere in Newman's work, above all in the Anglican parish sermons. And despite his rejection of ultramontanism, Newman seems unreflectingly ultramontane himself in equating the 'regal' or ruling function of the Church *tout court* with the papacy, without any mention of the episcopate at large. In the light of the theology of the Church embodied in the Second Vatican Council's Constitution on the Church, *Lumen Gentium*, the rigid separation he makes between the three offices or functions seems highly artificial and theologically malnourished. He shows no awareness in the *Preface* that the bishop at the liturgical heart of his church in the eucharist exercises all three functions of teaching, ruling and sacramental celebration. So, the *Preface* is woefully inadequate considered as a commentary on the scriptural or Patristic deployment of the triple offices of prophet, priest or king, whether in relation to the work of Christ or to the life of the Church.

Yet none of that was Newman's real concern: the

Preface addresses a different set of issues. His target was an understanding of the Church which was primarily authoritarian and managerial, and which tended to see the Church's teaching role as an aspect of rule, an attitude that has sometimes been waggishly summed up in the phrase 'Shut up, he explained'! In an age in which rigidly pyramidic and clericalist ecclesiologies prevailed, his intention was to argue for an irreducibly dialectical understanding of the life of the Church, to stress the plural nature of the elements of its life, and, not only to vindicate the legitimate role and freedom of theology as a permanent element in that dynamic, but to identify it, and not the governing or regal office, as the 'regulating principle' of the triad:

> I say then, Theology is the fundamental and regulating principle of the whole Church system. It is commensurate with Revelation, and Revelation is the initial and essential idea of Christianity. It is the subject-matter, the formal cause, the expression, of the Prophetical Office, and ... has created both the Regal Office and the Sacerdotal. And it has in a certain sense a power of jurisdiction over those offices, as being its own creations, theologians being ever in request and in employment in keeping within bounds both the political and popular elements in the Church's constitution.[114]

On Newman's account, the life of the Church could never be one of a sealed and self-sufficient balance, raising it above confusion, contradiction and error. It was a dialectical process, a perichoresis or dance of forces, rich and life-giving. John Coulson, one of the best commentators on the Preface, characterized its central notion as 'an equilibrium of functions' within the Church. But 'equilibrium' does not entirely reflect Newman's sense of the inevitabiity of tensions between the conflicting claims of truth, expediency and devotion. Despite his concession to the Ultramontanes that 'union and subordination', the concern of the regal office, were essential to the idea of the Church, he believed that these tensions would not be fully resolved this side of the eschaton.[115] As he wrote

> Whatever is great refuses to be reduced to human rule, and to be made consistent in its many aspects with itself. Who shall reconcile with each other the various attributes of the Infinite God? ... This living world to which we belong, how self-contradictory it is, when we attempt to measure and master its meaning and scope ... We need not feel surprise then, if Holy Church too, the supernatural creation of God, is an instance of the same law ... crossed and discredited now and again by apparent anomalies which need, and which claim, at our hands an exercise of faith.[116]

The *Preface* was not quite Newman's last significant theological utterance. If the definition of papal infallibility had been the issue that had most troubled him about the Vatican Council, he was also uneasy about the Council's ruling on the inspiration of scripture, which he took to be more restrictive than that adopted by the Council of Trent.[117] Newman believed (mistakenly) that whereas Trent had ruled that it was the writers of the Bible who were inspired, rather than the books they had written, the Vatican Council has defined that the books themselves were inspired, and therefore all they contained was literally true.[118] In Tract 85, written while he was still an Anglican, Newman had used the fact of the fallibility of historical and factual material in the Bible as an argument in favour of tradition and the authority of the Church, and he remained alert to the problems for faith posed by biblical criticism. In 1865 he had been visited at the Oratory by the liberal anglican Dean Stanley of Westminster, and they had discussed these issues. Newman told Stanley he had recognized the multiple authorship of the Pentateuch from his first reading of Genesis in Hebrew, and Pusey had conceded then that there was more than one author: 'would he do so now?'. Newman then went on to 'play the 'Devils' Advocate" against the story of David in the Books of Samuel, saying that it seemed 'more like a poem than any other part of the Bible'. And while Newman appeared to Stanley to be worried about applying this kind of 'dissolving criticism' to the Gospels, he admitted to Stanley that, 'I seem to myself to see this same compilatory character in the Gospels: not a regular history, but biographical anecdotes strung together.' But Newman considered all this was a problem for Protestants rather than Catholics, since Catholics relied on the Church's authority, and that authority had not so far defined that scripture (as distinct from the inspired authors of scripture) was itself inspired.[119]

Unsurprisingly, therefore, Newman was dismayed by what he thought was the Vatican Council's closing down what had formerly been open questions. He returned to this issue often in private notes, conversation and correspondence, but in 1884 he was moved to publish on the subject in response to an article in the *Nineteenth Century* magazine, which he believed misrepresented Catholic teaching on the subject. The gist of his argument was that the doctrine of the inspiration of scripture applied simply to matters of faith and morals, and was compatible with errors of historical fact (eg. the improbably immense ages of the patriarchs) or the attribution of books of the Bible to persons who had not in fact written them (eg. the so-called books of Moses, or the Pauline authorship of Hebrews), or the insertion of later material into the Gospels themselves (eg. the longer ending of St Mark, or the story of the woman taken in adultery in St John's Gospel).

Newman's views were contested both from within and outside the Catholic Church, most fiercely by Dr John Healy, a Maynooth professor and subsequently Archbishop of Tuam, who insisted on the literal truth of all biblical 'facts'. Both sides of the controversy have, of course, been overtaken by the transformation of biblical studies in the twentieth century, but Newman was writing a decade before the eruption of the Modernist crisis, and the consequent panicky closing down of serious Catholic biblical scholarship. His intervention was a characteristically careful attempt to leave open as many of the questions for faith raised by biblical criticism as possible, and to give Catholic biblical scholars room to explore and resolve those issues with freedom and intellectual integrity. Limited as the scope of his essay was, and cautious as was its tone, for a man in his eighties barely able to hold a pen, it was not far short of astonishing, and proof that his mind was questing, and unflinchingly honest, to the end

5
Man of letters

In 1850 Newman admonished one of his female correspondents against taking him for a saint: 'I have no tendency to be a saint – it is a sad thing to say, Saints are not literary men, they do not love the classics, they do not write Tales.'[120] It is a matter of interest that Newman in 1850 should think of himself as 'a literary man'. He had of course taught classics in Oxford, and the 'Tale' he refers to was his semi-autobiographical novel, *Loss and Gain: the story of a convert*, conceived while he was living in Rome, with the memory of his own conversion still strong upon him, and which was published anonymously in 1848. He had immediately begun another 'tale', this time an historical novel, *Callista*, set in third century ProConsular Africa. *Callista* was remarkable both for its vivid evocation of the plague of locusts which devastates the fictional city of Sicca in chapter ten, and for his heroine Callista's appeal, while still a pagan, to the voice of God in her conscience, 'the echo of a person speaking to me' that 'carries with it its proof of its divine origin ... An echo implies a voice; a voice a speaker. That speaker I love and I fear', a key element of Newman's thought, which he was to explore more formally in the *Grammar of Assent* and the *Letter to the Duke of Norfolk*.[121] Both novels still have life, and *Loss and Gain* is often very funny in a sub-

Dickensian way, but Newman was by any measure only a minor novelist.

There is more to be said for him as a poet: the novels are read primarily for the light they throw on Newman, but *The Pillar of the Cloud*, written aboard ship during his voyage back to England from Sicily in June 1833, has become one of the small handful of hymns that everyone has heard of, as 'Lead kindly light'. His most sustained poetic achievement, *The Dream of Gerontius,* written and published in 1865, is one of the best Victorian religious poems, theologically daring in its highly unconventional depiction of Purgatory as essentially the unfolding within the soul of Gerontius of his encounter with the holiness of God. The poem is metrically adventurous, and full of memorable phrasing, like Gerontius's description of the pangs of death:

> I can no more; for now it comes again,
> That sense of ruin, which is worse than pain,
> That masterful negation and collapse
> Of all that makes me man.[122]

The poem is also theologically adventurous, for, unlike most Victorian Catholic evocations of Purgatory, Newman's Purgatory is a 'golden prison', a place of healing and restoration. There is no fire there, and the bitterness of the 'penal waters' into which Gerontius' Guardian Angel lowers him 'softly and gently', to be tended and 'nursed' by willing angels, is the pain of penitence rather than of punishment. All the same, the *Dream* is as much a product of late romantic sensibility as of theological penetration. In the greatest of all poetic evocations of the Christian afterlife, Dante's *Commedia*, the vision of Purgatory is emphatically social, penitence and community are its twin themes, and the cleansing that takes place there involves the restoration of the justice and right order that sin destroys. By contrast, Gerontius in purgatory is 'lone, not forlorn', sinking far from all company into the lake of purgation, 'deeper, deeper into the dim distance' till the 'lone night watches' end, and the soul flies at last to 'its Sole Peace'. Here, as always in Newman, there are two and two only 'absolute and luminously self-evident beings, myself and my Creator'.[123] It demanded musical setting, and Elgar's sublime oratorio, which, as he famously declared, was 'the best of me' has ensured that Newman's sombrely beautiful meditation on the death, purgation and ultimate salvation of the soul of an ordinary man is one of the best-known of all Victorian poems. Two choruses from it, 'Praise to the Holiest' and 'Firmly I believe and truly' took on a life of their own in other musical settings, and rival the status of 'Lead kindly light' as classics of English hymnody. Despite a disastrously bad premier in Birmingham Town Hall in 1900, Elgar's work was soon recognized for the masterpiece that it is, though the blatantly Roman Catholic subject-matter raised Protestant hackles: to begin with it had to be performed at the Three Choirs Festival in a bowdlerized version.

But it is as the finest prose stylist of Victorian England, rivalled only by John Ruskin, that Newman's literary claims rest. James Joyce considered him beyond rivalry, and placed in the mouth of Stephen Dedalus on Sandymount strand a 'proud cadence' from what he elsewhere calls Newman's 'cloistral, silverveined prose'.[124]

Newman himself in fact disliked the idea of 'style'. Having been singled out in the *Times* of 10 April 1869 as one of the three great masters of English style (the others being Macaulay and de Quincy) he insisted that:

> I may truly say that I have never been in the practice since I was a boy of attempting to write well, or to form an elegant style. I think I never have written for writing sake; but my one and single desire and aim has been to do what is so difficult – viz. to express clearly and exactly my meaning.[125]

There was of course far more to Newman's writing than the search for clarity. He achieved fame as a stylist at first through his published *Parochial Sermons*, six volumes of them published between 1834 and 1842. Often treated as an undifferentiated body of perennial 'spirituality', divorced from the often hectic historical circumstances in which they were written and delivered, the sermons closely reflect Newman's own dramatic theological development in those years, but always underpinned by a consistently demanding emphasis on the search for holiness of life. Despite their austerity, the sermons won him a cult following among the young, and Victorian memoirs are full of recollections of the impact of his preaching. At the height of his fame as an Anglican, Newman often had to pick his way to the pulpit of St Mary's through hushed crowds of undergraduates, dons and visitors who came to Oxford 'principally to hear Newman preach'.

> 'Who could resist,' Matthew Arnold wrote in 1883, 'the charm of that spiritual apparition, gliding in the dim afternoon light through the aisles of St Mary's, rising into the pulpit, and then, in the most entrancing of voices, breaking the silence with words and thoughts which were a religious music – subtle, sweet, mournful.'

Equally impressive was the preacher's 'intensely tragic earnestness', his absolute stillness, eyes turned to the page before him, hands concealed behind the lectern, the long and at first disconcerting pauses between sentences, above all Newman's voice – calm, quiet, unemphatic, yet 'clear', 'sweet', 'thrilling', 'unearthly'.[126]

Newman's emphasis on communication and clarity meant that most of his sermons focussed on a single theme, signalled by their titles in the published versions – 'Secret Faults': 'Self Denial the Test of Religious Earnestness': 'Promising without Doing': 'The Self-Wise Enquirer'. And their style often embodied Newman's own stated preference for plain, direct, communication:

> Be in earnest, and you will speak of religion where, and when, and how you should; aim at things, and your words will be right without aiming. There are ten thousand ways of looking at this world, but only one right way. … it is the way in which God looks at the world. Aim at looking at it in God's way. Aim at seeing things as God sees them. Aim at forming judgments about persons, events, ranks, fortunes, changes, objects, such as God forms. Aim at looking at this life as God looks at it."[127]

Elsewhere, however, a wavering tentativness in his words might enact the uncertain process of human struggle for self-knowledge

> We are in the dark about ourselves. When we act, we are groping in the dark, and may meet with a fall any moment. Here and there, perhaps, we see a little; or, in our attempts to influence and move our minds, we are making experiments (as it were) with some delicate and dangerous instrument, which works we do not know how, and may produce unexpected and disastrous effects. The management of our hearts is quite above us.[128]

And despite his professed mistrust of conscious eloquence, his preaching often rises to the "subtle, sweet and mournful" musicality that Matthew Arnold remembered so admiringly after fifty years:

> But for us, let us glory in what they disown; let us beg of our Divine Lord to take to Him His great power, and manifest Himself more and more, and reign both in our hearts and in the world. Let us beg of Him to stand by us in trouble, and guide us on our dangerous way. … May He support us all the day long, till the shades lengthen, and the evening comes, and the busy world is hushed, and the fever of life is over, and our work is done! Then in His mercy may He give us safe lodging, and a holy rest, and peace at the last![129]

Read singly or in small groups, Newman's sermons are deeply affecting, often inspiring. But their almost unrelenting severity, their sense of the immense distance between the holiness of God and the deviousness of the human heart, have daunted many readers. Read in bulk they can be dispiriting, as many readers have felt: for Von Hugel, who admired the mind, Newman's religion was 'sad and sombre', a kind of puritanism, rooted in a temperamental defect. Looking back in 1921 on his youthful friendship with the aged Newman, 'I used to wonder', he wrote, 'how one so good, and who had made so many sacrifices to God, could be so depressing.'[130] As any reader of Newman's letters will know, this is an oversimplification, but the sermons do convey a severity that Newman's exalted theology of the divinization of human nature by the Christ's death and resurrection does not altogether offset. Yet their theological range is in fact extraordinary: most of Newman's abiding intellectual preoccupations found memorable expression not merely in his scholarly and argumentative writing, but in his preaching. Between the two world wars, the foremost promoter of Newman's thought in the German-speaking world, the Polish Jesuit Erich Przywara, compiled a hugely influential anthology of Newman's writings, the English version of which appeared in 1930 as *A Newman Synthesis*. The collection introduced thousands of readers in Europe, England and America to Newman's thought, though it suffers by removing Newman's ideas from the biographical framework which was so central to all his writing, and by extracting high moments of the prose from their argumentative context. Nevertheless, it is significant that Przywara drew by far the largest single block of his material from the ten volumes of Newman's Anglican sermons. It is hard to imagine a major corpus of Christian thought being derived nowadays from the parish sermons of any contemporary preacher.

The Idea of a University

The line from Newman that Stephen Dedalus recalled on Sandymount strand was indeed both 'silver-veined and cloistral' – it was the culminating sentence of Newman's perfervid evocation of the perpetual triumphs of the papacy, from the first of his *University Discourses*, Newman at his very lushest:

> Lawless kings arose, sagacious as the Roman, passionate as the Hun, yet in him they found their match, and were shattered, and he lived on. The gates of the earth were opened to the east and west, and men poured out to take possession; but he went with them by his missionaries, to China, to Mexico, carried along by zeal and charity, as far as those children of men were led by enterprise, covetousness, or ambition. Has he failed in

> his successes up to this hour? Did he, in our fathers' day, fail in his struggle with Joseph of Germany and his confederates, with Napoleon, a greater name, and his dependent kings, that, though in another kind of fight, he should fail in ours? What grey hairs are on the head of Judah, whose youth is renewed like the eagle's, whose feet are like the feet of harts, and underneath the Everlasting arms?[131]

Newman assembled the book from which that quotation came in 1873, by amalgamating nine of the ten discourses on *The Scope and Nature of a University Education* he had written as rector of the Catholic University of Ireland in 1852, and first published in 1853, supplemented by a series of ten further *Lectures and Essays on University Subjects*, first published in 1859. The resulting book, *The Idea of a University*, became almost at once a classic, and has remained the most widely read of all his works, endlessly reprinted and cited in every discussion of the nature and purpose of higher education: Walter Pater thought it 'the perfect handling of a theory', G. M. Young ranked it with Aristotle's *Ethics* and thought every other book on education could be pulped as redundant; Owen Chadwick thought that every University Vice-Chancellor should be made to pass an examination in it. Yet it has been often misunderstood. Because it has become the classic defence of liberal education, many of those most enthusiastic for it have had no interest in religion. Newman himself emphasized that his views on education were not derived fron theology, but from reflection on experience and 'imply no supernatural discernment'. Yet it is often overlooked that the lectures and the book derived from them were designed as a justification and explanation of the purpose of a Catholic University, in which the Church was an essential presence, in which all the professors were Catholics, and in which the value of a Catholic ethos was assumed.

Newman was addressing a very specific set of circumstances: the Irish hierarchy was divided over the wisdom and viability of an exclusively Catholic University, and Newman's defence of the value of knowledge for its own sake, and his insistence that it was not the task of a university to make good Catholics or Christians, was not necessarily in any case what any of them wanted to hear. The need to satisfy sometimes incompatible expectations led to some inconsistencies in his argument, like the claim in the seventh discourse that liberal education *was* after all useful, because it made good citizens.

The university, Newman suggested, was a community where all learning is taught: maintenance of 'the whole circle of the sciences' was essential to its being, and among the sciences he gave an important but not dominant place to theology: religion and knowledge of God was a fundamental aspect of human experience and history, and so could not be excluded from the circle of the sciences. This insistence reflected of course a life-long conviction, but was specifically directed here against the educational policy of the 'mixed education' of the non-denominational Irish 'Queens Colleges', from which theology was excluded, the government solution to the problem of educational provision in a country of fierce religious divisions.

Newman famously emphasized teaching as the university's principal function, insisting that it existed not primarily for research or training in practical skills, but a setting for the cultivation of intellect. This insistence has led to doubts about the relevance of Newman's vision to modern universities, where practical subjects like engineering, and cutting-edge research in the sciences are crucial, but the lectures do not in fact fully reflect Newman's vision of what was the appropriate scope of universities. As Rector, Newman built laboratories, encouraged his professors to do research, and created a research journal, *The Atlantis*, to publish their papers.

The fundamental role of university education, however, was not the transmission of facts, or the accumulation of mere knowledge, but to encourage 'enlargement of mind'. Its benefit was not utilitarian, its aim was to civilize. Fundamental to this process was the interchange of ideas and friendship found in the companionship of others, an issue which had been crucial for him during his time as an Oriel tutor. Newman went so far as to say he would prefer a university without professors, but where the students lived together and shared ideas, to a university where the students never encountered each other, but learned, for example, by correspondence courses. Newman was clear, however, about the limits of education:

> Knowledge is one thing, virtue is another. Good sense is not conscience, refinement is not humility … Liberal education makes not the Christian, not the Catholic, but the gentleman. It is well to be a gentleman, it is well to have a cultivated intellect, a delicate taste, a candid, equitable, dispassionate mind … these are the connatural qualities of a large knowledge: they are the objects of a University.

But

> Quarry the granite rock with razors, or moor the vessel with a thread of silk; then you may hope with such keen and delicate instruments as human knowledge and human reason to contend against those giants, the passions and the pride of man.[132]

Newman was echoing here the argument of his 1841 polemic on the *Tamworth Reading Room*: the inculcation of virtue was the province of the priest, not the professor. This distinction lay behind the famous and much-quoted portrait of the gentleman in the eighth discourse:

> It is almost the definition of a gentleman to say he is one who never inflicts pain … carefully avoids whatever may cause a jar or a jolt in the minds of those with whom he is cast – all clashing of opinion, or collision of feeling, all restraint, or suspicion, or gloom, or resentment; his great concern being to make every one at their ease and at home. He has his eyes on all his company; he is tender towards the bashful, gentle towards the distant, and merciful towards the absurd; he can recollect to whom he is speaking; he guards against unseasonable allusions, or topics which may irritate; he is seldom prominent in conversation, and never wearisome. He makes light of favours while he does them, and seems to be receiving when he is conferring. He never speaks of himself except when compelled, never defends himself by a mere retort, he has no ears for slander or gossip, is scrupulous in imputing motives to those who interfere with him, and interprets every thing for the best. He is never mean or little in his disputes, never takes unfair advantage, never mistakes personalities or sharp sayings for arguments, or insinuates evil which he dare not say out. From a long-sighted prudence, he observes the maxim of the ancient sage, that we should ever conduct ourselves towards our enemy as if he were one day to be our friend.

That has often been assumed to be Newman's ideal: it is in fact written with a strong element of irony, and is intended as a portrait of the best that nature without grace can achieve: this was refinement, not moral virtue. The irony becomes obvious when he moves on to the gentleman's religion:

> Not that he may not hold a religion too, in his own way, even when he is not a Christian. In that case his religion is one of imagination and sentiment; it is the embodiment of those ideas of the sublime, majestic, and beautiful, without which there can be no large philosophy. Sometimes he acknowledges the being of God, sometimes he invests an unknown principle or quality with the attributes of perfection. And this deduction of his reason, or creation of his fancy, he makes the occasion of such excellent thoughts, and the starting-point of so varied and systematic a teaching, that he even seems like a disciple of Christianity itself.

Newman concluded that discourse with pen-pictures of St Basil the Great and the emperor Julian the Apostate: both were 'gentlemen' formed by the same education, but 'one became a Saint and Doctor of the Church, the other her scoffing and relentless foe'.[133]

But he was equally insistent that the priest should not encroach on the prerogatives of the professor. No truth can contradict another truth, there was no final conflict between science and religion, even if in a given instance it is not at once apparent how they are to be reconciled. Scientific enquiry must be autonomous: the Church should learn from the Galileo affair to respect the legitimate freedom of scholars and scientists. And the Church should not seek to sanitize or censor what was studied in the university, neither in the sciences nor the arts. In the university, no area of knowledge was off bounds, and that included profane literature, for literature was by its nature profane:

> From the nature of the case, if Literature is to be made a study of human nature, you cannot have a Christian literature. It is a contradiction in terms to attempt a sinless literature of sinful man.[134]

The university was in the realm of ideas what an Empire was in the realm of politics, 'the high protecting power of all knowledge and science, of fact and principle … of experiment and speculation.' The 'imperial intellect' is therefore open to all knowledge, to the contradictions of experience and reality, accepting the complexities of life and knowledge even when they seem to involve conflict with religious truth. Unmistakeably echoing his own frustrations in the church of Pio Nono, he insisted on the need for believers – and church authorities – to avoid reaching for their revolvers every time a new idea was propounded. Pioneering thought pushes at the boundaries, 'Great minds need elbow room.'[135] So, the educated believer

> is not the nervous creature who startles at every sudden sound, and is fluttered by every strange or novel appearance … He is sure, and nothing shall make him doubt, that, if anything seems to be proved by astronomer, or geologist, or chronologist, or antiquarian, or ethnologist, in contradiction to the dogmas of faith, that point will eventually turn out, first, not to be proved, or, secondly, not contradictory, or thirdly, not contradictory to any thing really revealed … . And if, at the moment, it appears to be contradictory, then he is content to wait, knowing that error is like other delinquents; give it rope enough, and it will be found to have a strong suicidal propensity.[136]

Newman on himself

Among Newman's papers in the Birmingham Oratory is a scrapbook, containing some of his earliest letters and childhood memorabilia. By far the oddest item in that collection is the faded back cover of a school exercise book dating from 1812, when Newman was just eleven years old, and on which, then and at other key points over the course of his long life, he made a series of autobiographical jottings. They are terse enough to be quoted in their entirety.

> John Newman wrote this just before he was going up to Greek on Tuesday June 10th 1812, when it only wanted 3 days to his going home, thinking of the time (at home) when looking at this he shall recollect when he did it.
>
> At school now back again.
>
> And now at Alton where he never expected to be, being lately come for the vacation from Oxford where he dared not hope to be – how quick time passes and how ignorant are we of futurity. April 8th 1819, Thursday.
>
> And now at Oxford but with far different feelings – let the date speak – Friday February 16th 1821.
>
> And now in my rooms at Oriel College, a Tutor, a Parish Priest and Fellow, having suffered much, slowly advancing to what is good and holy, and led on by God's hand blindly, not knowing whither He is taking me. Even so, O Lord. September 7 1829. Monday morning ¼ past 10.
>
> And now a Catholic at Maryvale and expecting soon to set out for Rome. May 29, 1846.
>
> And now a Priest and Father of the Oratory, having just received the degree of Doctor from the Holy Father. September 23, 1850
>
> And now a Cardinal. March 2 1884."[137]

That extraordinary document bears a great deal of thinking about. Already in its first entry, at the age of eleven, Newman articulated what was to be one of the abiding characteristics of his life and psychology, the self-conscious brooding over his own past and its significance which would shape his most revealing writings. We wonder at the eleven-year-old schoolboy solemnly making the entry 'thinking of the time (at home) when looking at this he shall recollect when he did it', and some of Newman's other life-long preoccupations surface in these entries too, the fragility and uncertainty of human life and of human knowledge which dominate both his preaching and his epistemology, and that sense of moving blindly forward under God's guidance, familiar from his best known hymn, 'Lead Kindly Light'.

Regardless of content, the mere fact of these brief entries gives pause for thought. They were made over a period of seventy-two years, and record, sometimes long after the event, key moments in Newman's life – school days, the first Oxford vacation after his father's bankruptcy, his election as a Fellow of Oriel, his conversion to Catholicism, his establishment of the Oratory at Birmingham, and finally the Cardinalate. We have to imagine Newman hunting out or happening across this faded relic of his childhood as he pored over his papers at ever-increasing intervals – there's a gap of a few months between the first two entries, thirty-four years between the final two – in order to record (for whose eyes, one wonders?) yet another milestone in the fascinating unfolding of his own life. Here with a vengeance stands revealed that self-reflexive sensibility which, as he tells us in the *Apologia*, rested 'in the thought of two and two only absolute and luminously self-evident beings, myself and my Creator.'

Newman was, notoriously, a man intensely preoccupied by his own history and thought-processes. Henri Bremond, who admired him and wrote a perversely great book about him, called Newman 'one of the most self-absorbed men that has ever been known', and he dubbed that aspect of Newman's personality 'autocentrism', a word damningly though inadequately translated into English as 'self-centredness'.[138] He certainly was an incorrigible diarist, memoirist, letter-writer. Intensely and genuinely private, with a horror of glib confessional gab, he nevertheless wrote thousands of sometimes startlingly self-revealing letters to a wide circle of friends, many of them to women. More than 20,000 have survived (compared to Dickens' score of 14,000+) and have been printed in thirty-one large volumes, making Newman easily the most copious letter-writer, and probably the principle beneficiary, of the age of the penny post. As he told his sister Jemima, he himself considered that 'a man's life lies in his letters', and described them as

> just that kind of literature which more than any other represents the abundance of the heart, which more than any other approaches to conversation.[139]

Newman's letters allow us to eavesdrop on some of the most interesting and entertaining conversations of the nineteenth century. As even the scattering of passages from the letters quoted in this small book testify, the range of his correspondence is extraordinary: accounts of his travels (he disliked hotel food, especially continental hotel food, and hated soft beds): frenetic organization and campaigning (in the 1830s): family gossip: extended theological or philosophical reflections: analysis of church affairs: literary criticism and literary gossip: affectionate exchanges with close friends: and especially in his Catholic years, spiritual counsel and consolation, even a skittish rhyming thank you letter to a little girl who sent him cakes. He can be tender, businesslike, comical, piercingly intelligent, savagely critical. The letters are often moving, often painful, often very funny:

Newman had a strong sense of the ridiculous, and was good at catching the tone of a voice to comic effect. He could be devastatingly direct, as in his letter to Archbishop Manning in November 1869 when relations between them were at their worst: 'I do not know whether I am on my head or my heels, when I have active relations with you. In spite of my friendly feelings, this is the judgement of my intellect', or again, in his scathing rebuke to W. G. Ward in May 1867:

> You are doing your best to make a party in the Catholic Church, and ...dividing Christ by exalting your opinions into dogmas, and shocking to say, by declaring to me, as you do, that those Catholics who do not accept them are of a different religion from yours. I protest then again, not against your tenets, but against what I must call your schismatical spirit and I pray God that I may never denounce, as you do, what the Church has not denounced."[140]

And he could above all be profoundly touching. What is arguably his most moving letter was written in old age, soon after he became a Cardinal, to the son of his sister Jemima, who had died on Christmas Day 1879. Her family had never accepted Newman's conversion to Catholicism, and had been upset when he wrote to say he had offered Mass for her soul, but had not expressed a conventionally Victorian hope that he would meet her in the afterlife. Newman's explanation is as sublime as it is characteristically autocentric:

> My very dear John,
>
> Thank you for your affectionate letter, which I am glad to have, tho' how to answer it I scarcely know, more than if it were written in a language which I could not read. From so different a standpoint do we view things. Looking beyond

this life, my first prayer, aim, and hope is that I may see God. The thought of being blest with the sight of earthly friends pales before that thought. I believe that I shall never die; this awful prospect would crush me, were it not that I trusted and prayed that it would be an eternity in God's Presence. How is eternity a boon, unless He goes with it?

And for others dear to me, my one prayer is that they may see God. It is the thought of God, His Presence, His strength which makes up, which repairs all bereavements.

'Give what Thou wilt, without Thee we are poor,
'And with thee rich, take what Thou wilt away.'

I prayed that it might be so, when I lost so many friends 35 years ago; what else could I look to? If then, as you rightly remind me, I said Mass for your dear Mother, it was to entreat the Lover of souls that, in His own way and in His own time, He would remove all distance which lay between the Sovereign Good and her, His creature. That is the first prayer, *sine qua non*, introductory to all prayers, and the most absorbing. What can I say more to you?

Yours affectly
John H. Card. Newman
P.S. Cardinals don't wear mourning.[141]

The *Apologia*

That Newman's greatest literary achievement should be a spiritual autobiography is a matter for remark. This is in part because he was an intensely private man, with a shuddering horror of vulgar self-display, and an innate reticence and shyness which could keep him silent for hours in company. The *Apologia* itself begins by invoking that reticence 'It may easily be conceived how great a trial it is to me to write the following history of myself' he wrote, '...the words "*Secretum meum mihi*" keep ringing in my ears: but as men draw towards their end, they care less for disclosures.'[142] And yet the *Apologia* was full of disclosures: his childhood fears and superstitions, his awestruck admiration as a young don for his Oxford seniors, the making and the breaking of friendships, his fierce opinions and feverish campaigning in the heyday of the Oxford Movement, his hopes, his successes, his increasingly bitter disappointments, and the slow erosion of his once dominant position in the university and the wider Church of England.

But the *Apologia* was not primarily a narrative of events, unless we count shifts of mood, opinion and belief as events. The trigger for the book was Charles Kingsley's gratuitously insulting aside in a review of Froude's *History of England*, impugning Newman's integrity and truthfulness, and that of the Catholic priesthood in general. It seemed a heaven-sent opening. Newman had been deeply depressed, combing back through his papers and brooding on the frustrations that had blighted every enterprise since 1845.

> O how forlorn & dreary has been my course since I have been a Catholic! Here has been the contrast – as a Protestant I felt my religion dreary, but not my life – but as a Catholic, my life dreary, not my religion.[143]

Newman's response to Kingsley, published in eight pamphlets, concluded with a distressingly brilliant response in detail to his attack, arranged in thirty-nine sections in allusion to the thirty-nine articles. In it, all Newman's forensic and satirical powers were on display: friends and foes found it dazzling but savage, comparing it to a flaying, and Newman wisely suppressed it in later editions.[144] But the main part of his response was to invite the Victorian public in to view the workings of his innermost self, in vindication of his sincerity during his journey from Anglicanism to Catholicism:

> He asks what I mean: not about my words, not about my actions, … but about that living intelligence, by which I write, and argue, and act. He asks about my Mind and its Beliefs and Sentiments, and he shall be answered … I recognised what I had to do, though I shrank from both the task and the exposure which it would entail. I must, I said, give the true key to my whole life: I must show what I am that it may be seen what I am not … I wish to be known as a living man, and not as a scarecrow which is dressed up in my clothes..I will draw out, as far as may be, the history of my mind".[145]

But no-one was more aware than Newman of the problematic nature of any such history of a mind. The sources of belief and action are elusive, and to trace the origin of an idea or a motive is to try to cage the wind. Some of his most brilliant Anglican writing explored the quicksilver nature of motive and belief. In that sparkling and devastating attack on Victorian progressivism, *Letters on the Tamworth Reading Room* in 1840, he wrote that 'man is not a reasoning animal; he is a seeing, feeling, contemplating, acting animal.'[146] As we have seen, his *Oxford University Sermons* from the same period, developed a searching analysis of the roots of belief, and he set out there the impossibility of a complete account of the processes by which the mind arrives at its innermost convictions.

> It passes on from point to point, gaining one by some indication, another on a probability; then availing itself of an association; then falling back on some received law; next seizing on testimony; then committing itself to some

> popular impression, or some onward instinct, or some obscure memory; and thus it makes progress not unlike a clamberer on a steep cliff, who, by quick eye, prompt hand, and firm foot, ascends how he knows not himself, by personal endowments and by practice, rather than by rule.[147]

That sense of the elusiveness of mind and motive pervades the *Apologia*, especially in Newman's account of his last years in the Church of England, when, as he wrote 'I was on my death-bed, as regards my membership of the Anglican Church'.[148] From 1843 he was confiding to friends his increasing conviction that Rome was the one true Church, and Anglicanism in heresy and schism. Yet he clung to his membership of the Church of England, and till the autumn of 1845 did all in his power to hold back from Rome the group of ardent young disciples gathered round him in his retreat at Littlemore, that group unkindly but not entirely unjustly characterized by Geoffrey Faber as Newman's 'coterie of hermaphrodites'.

Newman's agonizingly prolonged intellectual and emotional journey towards Rome in those years baffled his contemporaries, who wondered why he dithered. Newman himself explained it in the *Apologia* in terms of his own religious epistemology. True conversion was no simple clear-cut matter of following logic, but involved a movement of heart and mind and will together, in a convergence which could neither be coerced or hurried, and which remained mysterious even to the convert himself.

> I had a great dislike of paper logic. For myself, it was not logic that carried me on: as well might one say that the quicksilver in the barometer changes the weather. It is the concrete being that reasons; pass a number of years, and I

> find my mind in a new place; how? The whole man moves; paper logic is but the record of it. All the logic in the world would not have made me move faster towards Rome than I did; as well might you say I have arrived at the end of my journey, because I see the village church before me, as venture to assert that the miles over which my soul had to pass before it got to Rome, could be annihilated … Great acts take time.[149]

The *Apologia* was an extraordinary physical and emotional feat, a sustained act of recollection and self-explanation, incorporating extracts from his letters of the time, many of them hastily begged for the purpose from their original recipients. The book was written section by section against the clock, for weekly serial publication, Newman standing at his desk for up to sixteen hours a day and once for twenty-two hours, frequently sobbing from emotion and exhaustion as he relived the climactic experiences of his Anglican career, the loss of his place in the university and with it the leadership of the movement he had helped create, and the partings with friends and family his conversion had involved. As late as 1862, Newman had been capable of writing dismissively and even savagely about his Anglican past: in a notorious letter to the *Globe* newspaper that year, to scotch rumours that he regretted his conversion and was planning to return to the Church of England, he had declared that 'the thought of the Anglican service makes me shiver, and the thought of the Thirty-nine articles makes me shudder.'[150]

Anglican friends and former followers had unerstandably been deeply hurt by those words: the *Apologia* made conscious amends by the warmth of his personal remembrances, his manifest sense of indebtedness to his Anglican past. That aspect of the *Apologia* was at its most moving, and in the best sense most artfully nostalgic, in the account of his final departure from Oxford after his reception as a Catholic:

> I left Oxford for good on Monday, February 23, 1846. I slept on Sunday night at my dear friend's, Mr. Johnson's, at the Observatory. Various friends came to see the last of me; Mr. Copeland, Mr. Church, Mr. Buckle, Mr. Pattison, and Mr. Lewis. Dr. Pusey too came up to take leave of me; and I called on Dr. Ogle, one of my very oldest friends, for he was my private Tutor, when I was an Undergraduate. In him I took leave of my first College, Trinity, which was so dear to me, and which held on its foundation so many who had been kind to me both when I was a boy, and all through my Oxford life. Trinity had never been unkind to me. There used to be much snapdragon growing on the walls opposite my freshman's rooms there, and I had for years taken it as the emblem of my own perpetual residence even unto death in my University.
>
> On the morning of the 23rd I left the Observatory. I have never seen Oxford since, excepting its spires, as they are seen from the railway.[151]

From the very first, most readers have felt that the *Apologia* succeeded in the almost impossible task of tracing Newman's tortuous journey towards certainty, and that his account of the workings of his own mind to 1845 carried and carry still the stamp of authenticity. Hostile Protestant reviewers might deplore Newman's Catholic opinions, but they recognized the psychological mastery with which he traced the journey by which he had arrived at them, and the literary mastery in which that journey was recounted. As one of them wrote:

> As a revelation of character the *Apologia* stands almost alone.. in the stern, judicial, unfaltering and unfearing self-analysis

> of it. While it reminds us of Augustine's *Confessions*, it is a far deeper revelation, and a far greater moral achievement than they.[152]

But there have always been sceptics, not least Newman's own brother Frank. Just one year after Newman's death, Frank published a venomous and fratricidal little memoir in which he vented the resentments and grudges of sixty years, and in which he dismissed the *Apologia* in particular as a disingenuous cover-up of his over-rated elder brother's real motives:

> 'The narrative of his religious changes would have deeply interested me,' he wrote, 'but I suppose he was incapable of writing it.'[153]

Francis Newman was an angular sectarian and a sceptic, who had despised his brother's Anglicansim even more than his later Catholicism, and he manifestly understood the inwardness of neither. But, unsurprisingly, other critics of the *Apologia* have been motivated by their own religious allegiances. For the Victorian broad-churchman Edwin Abbott, whose relentlessly disparaging though shrewd and well-informed two-volume study of *The Anglican Career of Cardinal Newman* remains in some ways the most formidable attack on the *Apologia*, Newman's narrative was a chronicle of self-deception, tracing the surrender of a first-class mind to irrationality and superstition.[154] For the Anglo-Catholic F. L. Cross, by contrast, the *Apologia* misled by giving too much weight to the intellectual case against Anglicanism, and presenting Newman's loss of faith in the theory of the *Via Media* as the reason for his conversion. The Tractarian experiment, Cross argued, had been in fact a success, and

Newman's abandonment of it in 1845 proceeded not from a realization of the inadequacy of its theological underpinning, but from his own temperamental shortcomings. He was, Cross argued, a prime example of the personality type characterized by Neitzsche by the term *Resentiment*: a slavish, submissive-aggressive personality type, backing down when confronted by strong opposition, while preserving self-respect by insisting on the possession of the high moral ground, and in the aftermath of defeat liable to wallow in self-pity and an abiding sense of grievance. According to Cross, it was his inability to cope with the hostile response to Tract 90, and the challenging of his influence within the Church of England, which forced Newman into retreat at Littlemore, and ultimately took him off in a huff to Rome.[155] Cross's critique of Newman's reasoning was manifestly *parti pris,* a defense of Anglo-Catholicism by an Anglo-Catholic, but he had certainly put his finger on aspects of Newman's character which leap from the pages of his collected correspondence. Newman was, notoriously, a man without a skin, hyper-sensitive to criticism and opposition, one slow to forgive or forget once offended.

A less existentially engaged sense than Cross's that the *Apologia* might be misleading, however, surfaced among historians conscious that Newman's book had stamped an indelible mark on the historiography of the Oxford Movement, and had thereby distorted perceptions both of the context of the Movement and of Newman's own role within it. The classic account was Richard Church's *The Oxford Movement*, first published in 1891 and still a standard point of reference.[156] Church, as a junior Fellow of Oriel from 1838, had been a devoted disciple, and remained a close friend till Newman's death. Church's study of early Tractarianism is full of insight as well as information, but it places Newman centre-stage, at the expense both of other Tractarian leaders like Keble and Pusey, and of the movement's spreading influence outside the university. Above all perhaps, it ends abruptly in 1845, with Newman's secession. Church's book closely follows the narrative framework of the *Apologia*, and his omissions and silences are also derived from his master. Newman had said very little, for example, about some of his major polemical preoccupations in the 1830s, in particular his running battle with early Victorian Evangelicalism, which loomed far larger in his Tractarian preaching and writing than anyone would suspect from reading the *Apologia* alone: Church is equally silent on this score, and on the rare occasions when he does mention Evangelicalism, it is clear that he shared Newman's strong aversion to it.

For a generation or more, therefore, historians have been increasingly aware of the need to escape from the narrative stereotypes fixed by Newman's masterpiece of persuasion, and to present a less idealized and less sanitized account of a movement which was both more various and more pugnacious than his account suggested. This has resulted in some bracingly revisionist work. Perhaps the most substantial was Peter Nockles' magisterial *The Oxford Movement in Context*, which rehabilitated the High Church predecessors of the Oxford Movement from Tractarian disparagement. In the same vein was the 1999 essay by Simon Skinner, which uncovered Newman's ruthless hijacking of the *British Critic*, the stiffly old-fashioned periodical managed by members the High Church movement known as the Hackney Phalanx. Skinner showed that, having deviously ousted the existing editor, Newman transformed the *Critic* into a much more pugnacious platform for advanced Tractarian views. Yet, though his work as editor absorbed a good deal of his energy and enthusiasm for three years at the height of the movement's success, Newman devoted just seven lines to the *British Critic* in the *Apologia*, said nothing about his own ousting of his predecessor as editor, and played down the extent to which the magazine under his management became very much the Tractarian in-house journal. 'My writers', he claimed, 'belonged to various schools, some to none at all'.[157] In reality, Newman carefully vetted his contributors, and refused offers of copy from men like Samuel Wilberforce whom he did not trust to toe the Tractarian party line.[158]

Skinner's study brought a refreshingly acerbic note to the often reverential tone of much Newman scholarship, but he was primarily concerned to set the record straight on a key episode in the history of Tractarianism, rather than to offer a sustained critique of Newman's own subsequent presentation of the origins and character of Tractarianism. As we have seen, the *Apologia* was written for weekly serial publication, under extreme pressure of time. At a distance of twenty-five years, Newman's recollection of his criteria for selection of writers for the B*ritish Critic* may well have been hazy, but in any case that kind of detail was not germane to his apologetic purpose. Chapter 2 of the *Apologia* contained a very frank confession of the deviousness and ferocity which 'absolute confidence in my cause' led to in the early 1830s, and he probably felt that that admission sufficiently covered his ruthless behaviour over the editorship of the *British Critic*.

But it is all the same not so easy to absolve him of disingenuousness in the final chapter of the *Apologia* . Entitled *Position of my mind since 1845*, that part of the *Apologia* represents a significant change of style and purpose. We move from a compelling psychological analysis of Newman's journey towards Catholicism, to a more straightforwardly apologetic defence of the Catholic Church in which that journey had ended. But 'straightforward' is in this case is not entirely the apt description. As we have seen, this final section of the *Apologia* contains some of his most compelling and eloquent writing.[159] But it also contains startling evidence that a text by Newman may not be all it purports to be. One of the central Protestant opinions Newman sets out to confute is the notion that obedience to an infallible authority 'destroys the independence of the mind', to which he replies that 'the whole history of the Church … gives a negative to the accusation.' Newman justifies this claim by describing how in the middle ages theological ideas had been freely advanced, debated and quarrelled over, so that only after years or even centuries of discussion did Rome reluctantly move to resolve the dispute with a final decision. This leisurely process by which new theological claims are aired and tested, he wrote, 'tends not only to the liberty, but to the courage, of the individual theologian or controversialist.' For no-one would dare to do speculate if they knew that 'an authority, which was supreme and final, was watching every word he said, and made signs of assent or dissent to each sentence, as he uttered it. Then indeed he would be fighting, as the Persian soldiers, under the lash, and the freedom of his intellect might truly be said to be beaten out of him. *But this has not been so*.'[160]

To anyone familiar with Newman'sprivate correspondence in the 1860s, the phrasing of that denial has a disturbing familiarity: his description of the process by which theological ideas are sifted in the Church is almost word for word the mirror-image of his bitter complaints to friends like Emily Bowles about the repression threatening any theological venture under Pio Nono. He himself claimed specifically that he was writing 'under the lash'.[161] His harsh analysis of the sterility and oppression of the theological scene in contemporary Catholicism is turned on its head in the final section of the *Apologia*, to claim that there was unhindered intellectual freedom in the Church, a freedom whose very existence he was almost simultaneously bitterly denying in private. Newman's motives here are of course easy enough to explain: from the publication of the *Idea of a University* onwards, he had been consciously promoting, to Catholics as much as to Protestants, an understanding of Catholicism as open and confident enough to absorb and make use of all that was good in contemporary culture. Hence his insistence that hyper-Catholics like Manning, Ward and Faber were 'in no sense spokesmen' for the Church.[162] He believed (probably rather optimistically) that 'in former times' theological issues had been left mainly to the 'schools', that is, the theologians, with authority intervening only at last and when called upon. In maintaining that this was the normative situation in the Church, Newman was as much making an act of faith and hope as a description of present reality: ultramontanism would pass, and another age, another pope, another council, would 'trim the boat'.

There was another and more personal dimension to all this. Newman consistently deferred to papal authority in all his published writings: however angrily critical he felt privately, his deference to papal authority meant his only public form of protest was silence. It was an aspect of his personality which enraged John Acton and disturbed Von Hugel who, at the height of the Modernist Crisis in 1911 told Newman's biographer, Wilfred Ward, that Newman's silences represented a 'grave peculiarity and defect of the Cardinal's temper of mind and position'. Never to allow 'any public protestation … act or declaration contrary to current Roman policy …. would stamp Our Lord himself as a deplorable rebel … would condemn St Paul at Antioch … and censure many a great saint of God since then.'[163] But whatever Newman's motivation in refraining from direct public criticism of the papacy, whether by principle or temperament, he was well aware that what he was claiming in the final section of the *Apologia* about the freedom of the theologian was not a present fact: in this respect, at least, he was being less than honest with his readers.

A charge of dishonesty had triggered the *Apologia* in the first place, and the charge would never entirely go away. Newman's honesty was subjected to hostile analysis from within the Catholic Church in 1969 in a pseudonymously published book, *Apologia Pro Charles Kingsley* by 'G. Egner' (German, 'opponent'). The pseudonym concealed the identity of a formidably learned Roman Catholic priest-philosopher, Fr P. J. Fitzpatrick, who had originally adopted the name when he published a book against the encyclical *Humane Vitae*. The title of his fiercely entertaining book summarizes its content.[164] But the most sustained modern onslaught on the integrity and accuracy of the *Apologia* was a massive 700 page study of Newman's Anglican career by the Yale historian, the late Frank Turner.[165] Turner argued that in the *Apologia* Newman had systematically created a smokescreen to obscure and distort the truth about his early life, and about the nature of the Tractarian movement in general. Newman had claimed in the *Apologia* that his battle in the 1830s, and ever since, had been with what he called 'liberalism', an elusive concept which roughly speaking meant rationalism and the use of private judgement in matters of religion, which itself was viewed as a sentiment rather than a body of truth: to this,

Newman opposed the dogmatic principle and the authority of Catholic tradition. But this emphasis,Turner argued, reflected the pressing needs of the Catholic Newman in the era of the *Syllabus of Errors*, not the realities of the Anglican Newman of the 1830s and 40s. The battle with liberalism he believed was projected retrospectively on to the Tractarian Newman by the Catholic Newman, to deflect suspicions at Rome and among English ultramontanes like Manning that Newman was in fact guilty of excessive liberalism himself.

Newman's real obsession in the 1830s and 1840s, according to Turner, had been the battle against Protestant evangelicalism, and the Tractarian movement as a whole was far more accurately seen as anti-evangelical than as opposed to the hazy and elusive phantom of 'liberalism'. For Turner, therefore, the Anglican Newman was not the consistently evolving Catholic mind portrayed in the *Apologia*, but 'vulnerable, confused, contradictory, disingenuous, morbidly introspective and manipulative, an aggressive religious activist by whose often dazzling rhetoric posterity should not have been fooled.'[166] Turner was writing a decade before Newman's beatification, but he was conscious of assailing a cultural and religious icon, and he was careful to insist that his work was not directed at the later Newman of the *Apologia* and the *Dream of Gerontius*, nor against the saintly Cardinal. The 'protagonist' of his book was the fierce Anglican Newman of the 1830s and 1840s. And this J. H. Newman he portrayed as a contemptible creature, a dishonest, self-serving bigot, driven by spite, animosity, and 'explosive rage'. His attacks on liberal former friends and colleagues like Edward Hawkins and Richard Whately, and on the allegedly heretical Dr Renn Dickson Hamden, according to Turner had less to do with their alleged liberalism than with his enraged envy at their prosperity: 'without exception, those whom he associated with latitudinariansim and liberalism … were those whose career advancement had blocked or gone beyond his.'[167] And his 'enormous anger and spite' towards liberals in the Oriel Common-room 'to no small extent' paralleled those 'towards his [own] family', especially his brothers Charles and Frank.[168] Turner's Newman was sexually dysfunctional, and obsessed with celibacy. He gathered around him a group of unmarried male disciples, and it was the overwhelming need to hold on to this adoring circle of celibate younger men which provided the real motivation both for Newman's long drawn out years at Littlemore, postponing conversion to Rome, and then precipitating his apparently sudden conversion in October 1845, Newman's impatient disciples had one by one decided to join the Catholic Church, and Newman, according to Turner, eventually realized that if he himself didn't bite the bullet and become a Catholic he would cease 'to be the centre of their attention and affection'.[169] The anguished self-analytical letters of those last years as an Anglican, drawn on heavily in the *Apologia*, were therefore not a sign of real unsettlement, for Newman 'had taken himself to a brink over which he had no real desire to step.' They were, rather, exercises in attention-seeking, a characteristically devious way for Newman 'to intrude himself into the lives of a whole series of people … who might otherwise not necessarily be thinking very much about him.'[170] Newman's religion was 'utterly joyless', his excessive fasting and that of his disciples an eating disorder, a form of male anorexia, springing from a 'body-hating misogyny'. [171] Even Newman's sublimely austere *Parochial and Plain Sermons*, with their daunting emphasis on the moral and spiritual demands of Christian discipleship, sprang from a deep animosity towards his wayward brothers

Charles and Frank, and 'expressed a profound personal wish that within his family his own obedience might receive praise and the wilfulness of his brothers be condemned.'[172] Turner consolidated this devastating picture of the Anglican Newman with a new edition of the *Apologia* in 2008, with a lengthy introduction recycling the main contentions of the earlier book.

Reviewers in the secular broadsheet press were delighted with what they saw as a bracing exercise in iconoclasm, enjoying the sight and sound of an historical 'sledge-hammer' being wielded with 'panache'.[173] Turner's manifest distaste for many aspects of Tractarianism, his consistently disparaging portrait of the young Newman as a vindictive and spiteful narcissist, and his speculations about the submerged Freudian impact of Newman's famiiy relationships and friendships on his actions and ideas, all evoked distressed or furious responses, and the imminence of Newman's beatification served to raise the temperature. Turner had hedged with qualification his more outrageous speculations about the nature of Newman's male friendships. But these fig-leaf provisos were swept aside in media debates about Newman's sexuality, triggered by the vociferous opposition of the Gay Rights activist Peter Tatchell to the exhumation to recover Newman's relics from the grave he shared with his friend and disciple Ambrose St John,[174] and the beatification in September 2010.

One of the genuine merits of Turner's book was his recovery of the centrality of resistance to evangelicalism as a key to Newman's concerns in the 1830s. The relative silence about this preoccupation in the *Apologia* had been largely replicated in the subsequent scholarship, and Turner did a real service by his careful documentation of the Anglican Newman's pervasive anti-evangelicalism. But he pursued this genuine insight into a denial of the significance of any other targets in Newman's critique of Protestantism. Newman repeatedly made it clear that his detestation of evangelicalism sprang largely from his conviction that its emphasis on religious feeling, and neglect of ecclesial structures and the credal elements of Christianity, opened the door to rationalistic unbelief, what he came to characterize as *liberalism*. Newman made this connection repeatedly in the 1830s: as he told the evangelical layman Lord Lifford in September 1837, he hoped that the outcry against the alleged heresies of the liberal Dr Hamden would open evangelical eyes to the liberalizing tendency of their opinions: 'that system has become rationalistic in Germany, Socinian in Geneva … it tends to Socinianism among our own evangelical party.'[175] As Turner himself notes, Newman found vivid confirmation of that slide from evangelicalism to rationalism and unbelief in the career of his own brother Frank, whose journey from sectarian evangelicalism to Unitarian confirmed his worst fears about the underlying tendency of evangelical principles.[176]

Other Tractarian leaders also interpreted the theological conflicts of the 1830s ultimately, as John Keble remarked, as a struggle between 'Faith and Rationalism'.[177] Newman lampooned the vulgarities and superficiality of popular evangelicalism in his novel *Loss and Gain*, in the portraits of Mr Gabb and Mr Mackanoise – but he believed that its real danger lay in its unwitting collaboration in the headlong progress towards infidelity of which the optimistic religion of the day was another and quite different symptom. As he was to declare in the wake of the Gorham judgement in 1850, evangelicals might preen themselves in the belief that the spirit of the age was with them, but their success was only because they offered no resistance to that spirit, 'they glide forward rapidly and proudly down the stream', a stream flowing inevitably into a vast sea of unbelief.[178]

By 1864 the place of Evangelicalism within Anglicanism was of course no longer for Newman a matter of existential urgency, and he had also tempered his initial convert's zeal for direct confrontation with what in 1850 he had called 'that imbecile inconsistent thing called Protestantism'. The distressingly shrill 'convertitis' which make his polemical lectures on the *Present Position of Catholics*, for all their rumbustuous satire, such a painful read, gave way in the *Apologia* to a far warmer and more positive assessment of his Anglican years. But in 1864 he saw the same fundamental struggle going on between dogmatic religion and rank unbelief as in the 1830s, but now even more starkly defined: 'In these latter days,' he wrote, 'outside the Catholic Church things are tending ... to atheism in one shape or another.'[179] It was perfectly natural that in reviewing his own religious journey, Newman should highlight the struggle with anti-dogmatic Liberalism rather than with its epiphenomenon, Evangelicalism, as the key to his own life's deeper continuities. Certainly the *Apologia* is a product of 1864, not 1834: Newman could hardly write about the intellectual continuities in his journey towards Catholicism without taking colouring from his experience of and in that Church. His emphasis in the *Apologia* on his perfectly genuine life-long opposition to 'liberalism' undoubtedly had a strategic element, coloured by concern about the repressive ethos of Pio Nono's papacy. But to treat the relative lack of emphasis on Evangelicalism in the *Apologia* as a smokescreen seems a crassly reductive characterization of one of the world's masterpieces of confessional writing.

6
Legacy

Newman died a prince of the Church and, somewhat improbably, an English national treasure, eulogized in the *Spectator* as 'the great Anglican, the great Catholic, the great Englishman.' The *Times* printed a suggestion that Newman's hymn 'Lead kindly light' should be sung in tribute in every Protestant Church on the Sunday after his death, an Anglican dignitary even suggested a funeral in Westminster Abbey.[180] And his old foe, Cardinal Manning, preaching at a requiem Mass in the Brompton Oratory, placed Newman '… among the greatest of our people, as a confessor for the faith, a great teacher of men, a preacher of justice, of piety, and of compassion.'[181]

But despite all that, Newman's distinctive ideas had been neither understood nor widely accepted within the Catholic Church. The development of doctrine had indeed been invoked as justification for the definition of the Immaculate Conception in 1854, and to Newman's vexation was also used to justify the definition of papal infallibility in 1870: 'It has been my fate,' he complained to his friend Bishop Moriarty, 'to have my book attacked by various persons, praised by none – till at last it is used against me.'[182] But Cardinal Manning privately thought Newman's writings were a school of heresy, and suspicion, or worse, ignorance of Newman was widespread among the scholastically trained theologians in favour at Rome. To men convinced that 'the Catholic Church alone can challenge the world to point out a single inconsistency in her teaching, or a single weak point in the perfect system of divine Philosophy which God through her has given to the world,' the subtle and exploratory teaching of the *Oxford University Sermons* or the *Grammar of Assent* was bound to seem a subjective retreat on defective logic, the 'illative sense' a high-falutin' way of dressing up sloppy emotionalism.[183] Leo XIII's promotion of Thomas Aquinas as the model of Catholic theology encouraged the growth of a late nineteenth century neo-scholasticism which understood theology as bringing hard deductive reasoning to bear on revealed assertions, with no place for the 'personal conquest of truth', and no account of the preparation of the heart for truth, that Newman believed was the essence of faith. The result was a prevailing 'supernaturalized rationalism' in which 'immobility in practice and immutabilty in belief' became the twin faces of the theology favoured by the papacy.[184]

But there were many Catholics who felt the inadequacy of such a mindset as a response to the challenges to faith posed by modern philosophy, the natural and social sciences, and by historical and biblical studies. For such 'Liberal' Catholics, in France as well as England, the *Essay on Development* seemed to offer the key to an accommodation between modernity and the Church. And in Newman's marginalizing of external evidences as a starting point for faith, in favour of an emphasis on the role of conscience, and his account of 'the Illative sense' in the *Grammar*, many in the 1890s recognized an account of religious belief which assigned a vital place to human experience, intuition and imagination, dimensions of faith ignored or denied by the official theology.

French perception of Newman was coloured by the brilliant but misleading interpretation placed on his life and writings by Newman's most ardent French student, Henry Bremond, who saw the Newman of the *Grammar of Assent* as a fideist, hostile to human reason: Newman's emphasis on 'conscience, Christian experience and personal realization of the divine' made him, for Bremond, an English Schleiermacher, basing religion on personal feeling: for good and ill, that picture of Newman was widely believed. More nuanced and accurate presentations of the *Essay on Development* and the *Grammar of Assent* were mobilized by Alfred Loisy and George Tyrrell, whose attempts to reformulate Catholicism for an age of criticism nevertheless moved both of them away from an understanding of the deposit of faith as in any sense propositional, towards the canonization of subjective religious experience as the fundamental content of an ongoing revelation, whose successive doctrinal formulations were liable not merely to development, but to supercession. In the process they parted company with Newman, in Tyrrell's case to an explicit repudiation of the very idea of doctrinal development itself.[185]

Inevitably, this theological ferment triggered a reaction from the authorities, in which Newman himself seemed to be targeted. In January 1901 a joint pastoral letter against 'Liberal Catholicism', signed by all the English and Welsh bishops, tried to close down theological discussion with a distinction between the 'ecclesia docens' and the 'ecclesia discens' so stark as to make it seem that Newman's *Rambler* essay on consulting the laity was in their sights.[186] Worse was to follow. In July 1907 the profoundly anti-intellectual Pope Pius X, having excommunicated Loisy, issued a syllabus of current errors, *Lamentabili sanu exitu*, drawn mainly from the writings of Loisy and Tyrrell, and in September this was followed by an encyclical, *Pascendi dominici gregis*, denouncing 'Modernism' as the synthesis of all the heresies and inaugurating an authoritarian clamp-down on anything savouring of theological novelty.

Both documents seemed to target ideas associated with Newman, under the general heading of 'subjectivism' in matters of faith. The Fathers of the Birmingham Oratory hurried to secure a statement from Rome that Newman's views were not in fact being condemned, which of course made everyone suspect that they were. A panic-stricken Wilfred Ward, hard at work on his hero Newman's biography, was certain of it, and told the Duke of Norfolk that 'to maintain that the Encyclical does not say what it does will make things worse.' Gleefully Tyrrell published a series of letters and articles insisting that Newman, despite being 'an incurable ecclesiasticist' had forged in the *Essay* and the *Grammar of Assent* weapons which the Modernists were now using in their fight against scholasticism, 'Not in his scope or motive, but his method, Newman is the father of Modernists.'[187]

In fact Fr Joseph Lemius, who drafted the encyclical, had never read a word of Newman, and was working at the instigation of Pius X's Secretary of State, Cardinal Merry del Val, who greatly admired Newman. But Tyrrell's judgement contained an uncomfortable kernel of truth, and the effect of the Modernist crisis was to slow the reception of Newman's thought into Catholic theology for a whole generation, since most of those who defended Newman did so by downplaying the distinctiveness of his ideas and assimilating them to the current orthodoxy: so an American study of Newman's epistemology in 1918 could make the bizarre claim that Newman's theory of knowledge was 'in all essentials the same as that of the scholastics.'[188]

But between the two world wars Newman's works became better known, with good German translations of the *Essay on Development* and the *Grammar of Assent* appearing in 1920 and 1921. The revival of German Catholic theology in those years was spearheaded by men like Erich Przywara, Romano Guardini and Karl Adam, all of whom were appreciative readers of Newman, concerned to complement (or offset) the 'objective' theology of St Thomas with the psychological understanding of the nature of faith they found in *The Grammar of Assent*. As Przywara wrote, 'Newman's epistemological difficulties were the same as ours, he understood our historical situation and also what is going on in our hearts.'[189] This interest in Newman would blossom after 1945 in the generation of theologians who were to shape the theology of the Second Vatican Council and its aftermath, in Karl Rahner's and Bernard Lonergan's intense interest in the *Grammar of Assent*,[190] but perhaps above all in the movement known as the *Nouvelle theologie*, and the work of Yves Congar, for whom Newman's *Essay on Development* was a seminal text. Cardinal Joseph Ratzinger has recorded his own early exposure to Newman's work as a seminarian at Freising in the immediate aftermath of the Second World War:

> For us at that time, Newman's teaching on conscience became an important foundation for theological personalism, which was drawing us all in its sway. Our image of the human being as well as our image of the Church was permeated by this point of departure. We had experienced the claim of a totalitarian party, which understood itself as the fulfilment of history and which negated the conscience of the individual. One of its leaders had said: "I have no conscience. My conscience is Adolf Hitler". The appalling devastation of humanity that followed was before our eyes.

> So it was liberating and essential for us to know that the "we" of the Church does not rest on a cancellation of conscience, but that, exactly the opposite, it can only develop from conscience.[191]

Later, in Munich, he would deepen his acquaintance with the *Grammar of Assent*, and, through the work of Heinrich Fries, would study the *Essay on Development*, 'which I regard along with his doctrine on conscience as his decisive contribution to the renewal of theology.' Newman's name was seldom invoked during the debates at Vatican II, but some of the Council's key theological and ecclesiological concerns derive ultimately from his example, most obviously the recognition given to the role of the laity and the *sensus fidelium* in the life of the Church in the Dogmatic Constitution on the Church, *Lumen Gentium*, in the formal acceptance of the idea of doctrinal development in paragraph 8 of the Constitution on Revelation, *Dei Verbum* and in the Council's dramatic recasting of Roman Catholic teaching on Mary in scriptural and patristic terms in the final chapter of *Lumen Gentium*.

Newman was not an ecumenist: he envisaged the goal of Christian unity as a 'return' of schismatic or heretical Christians to the unity of Rome: as Vincent McNabb remarked, what 'began in the common-room at Oriel … can end only under the dome of St Peter's.'[192] A crucial aspect of his legacy, nevertheless, was his profound impact on the ecumenical movement, and not only on relations between the churches of Canterbury and Rome. A key text here was the *Lectures on Justification*. Those lectures purported to contrast Luther's teaching with that of the Roman Catholic Church, and Newman's exposition of Catholic teaching in them was considered by Hans Kung to be 'one of the best treatments of the Catholic theology of Justification.'[193] But Newman equated Luther's teaching on Justification with that of popular nineteenth century Evangelicalism and laid the faults he saw in that system at Luther's door: 'He found Christians in bondage to their works and observances; he released them by his doctrine of faith; and he left them in bondage to their feelings.'[194] Whatever the inadequacies of Newman's account of Luther's teaching, however, the *Lectures on Justification* struck out in a new direction by placing the indwelling presence of Christ through the Spirit as the agent and meaning of Justification. 'Uncreated grace', and the role of the Spirit in communicating the divine presence, had been neglected in both Protestant and Catholic thinking: Newman's introduction of a Trinitarian and Christological dimension to talk about Justification was a theological insight which would bear ecumenical fruit in modern Lutheran-Catholic dialogue.[195]

That Christological emphasis was the fruit of Newman's patristic studies. In the same way, his recasting in the *Letter to Pusey* of conventional Catholic Mariology, away from the decadent Baroque paradigms reflected in works like St Alfonso *Ligouri's Glories of Mary*, into a more patristic form, anticipated both the strategies of the *nouvelle theologie*, and the Mariology of the Second Vatican Council, and opened the way for fruitful ecumenical engagement between Catholics and Protestants on the role of Mary in the order of salvation.

But Newman's most significant contribution to ecumenism was himself: in becoming a Catholic, Newman repudiated none of the modes of thinking he had acquired as an Anglican, and those modes of thinking would in due course fertilize the theology of the Church into which he carried them. Manning's complaint that Newman represented 'the old

Anglican patristic, literary tone transplanted into the Church' was absolutely right, and it was precisely those features of his thought that gave Newman's thought freedom from the scholastic rigidities that were sterilizing the theology of his adopted Church. He was perfectly aware of the continuities in his own thinking, but there has been surprisingly little recognition of just how astonishing it is that a priest in an age when the Catholic Church was morbidly hostile to other Christian traditions should systematically set about republishing all his Protestant writings, with only minor alterations.

Newman is a complex figure, and his legacy is almost impossible to characterize simply. Pope Benedict found in Newman's writings on Conscience not the question mark against the exaggerations of power that Newman intended, but an endorsement of authority: as he explained in 1990,

> It was from Newman that we learned to understand the primacy of the Pope. Freedom of conscience, Newman told us, is not identical with the right "to dispense with conscience, to ignore a Lawgiver and Judge, to be independent of unseen obligations". Thus, conscience in its true sense is the bedrock of Papal authority; its power comes from revelation that completes natural conscience, which is imperfectly enlightened.[196]

Warrant for every word of that can of course be found in the *Letter to the Duke of Norfolk*. Yet, it is not the most obvious reading of the text. As this book has tried to show, in the church of Pio Nono Newman was an angular and uncomfortable figure, ill at ease with authority as it was actually exercised, fighting with all his immense intelligence and mastery of words to preserve 'elbow-room' for original thought, even where that might lead into uncharted territory, patient with those who were troubled or doubting, yet also a passionate believer in the objectivity of Christian truth and the right and obligation of the Catholic Church to declare and interpret it. Those tensions were fundamental to his thought, but they puzzled and on occasion antagonized those with less patience with ambiguity and incompleteness. In 1861, he jotted down in one of his theological notebooks, 'It is very inexpedient for oneself to go as near the wind as possible in faith, but it is very wrong not to open the necessary faith as wide as possible for others.'[197] That remark captures the generosity of intelligence that motivated Newman's detestation of slick answers to hard questions. Donald McKinnon spoke appreciatively of Newman's 'subtle, exploratory intelligence', and John Coulson of the 'note of interrogation' that characterized his epistolary style.[198] Lord Acton, a man of absolutes, moved from awed admiration of Newman as a defender of freedom of thought in the Church, to outrage and detestation that 'the venerable Noggs' had first resisted but then accepted the Vatican Council's definition of Papal Infallibility. Newman's caution, his refusal to opt for black and white solutions and outright statements, irritated Acton, he thought Newman was always covering his back. But, though in a more hostile key, he too noted the same exploratory character of Newman's mind, 'fervid, anxious and unresting … so intense, so little of the rank and file, his mind so subtle, so dexterous, so original.'[199]

The canonization of Newman is no conventional accolade to a very pious man. Newman strove all his life after holiness, but he had more than his share of human frailties. He could be tyrannical in friendship, he was thin-skinned and easily offended, slow to forgive, even at times implacable. Canonizations always have a point, which is often political, in the broadest sense. Newman believed passionately that religion without dogma slid inexorably into mere sentiment, and it would be possible to portray him as the patron saint of dogmatism, a model for the tame theologian anxiously eager to stay within the bounds of orthodoxy. But that would be a radical misunderstanding of his life's work. Newman possessed one of the most original Christian minds of modern times, indeed of any time. His significance for the Catholic Church, and for all the churches, is neither as a model of mere piety, nor as a paragon of conformist orthodoxy, but specifically as a teacher and exemplar of Christian thinking at the edge, for the patient, generous, attentive and interrogative mind he brought to bear on the questions of good and evil, meaning and purpose, that are the heart of religion. Gifted with a radiant intelligence, he had an intense distrust of mere intellect. Towards the end of the *Grammar of Assent*, he wrote, 'I do not want to be converted by a smart syllogism; if I am asked to convert others by it, I say plainly I do not care to overcome their reason without touching their hearts. I wish to deal not with controversialists, but with inquirers.' Newman adopted as his cardinalatial motto the phrase 'Heart speaks to heart'. By both heart and head, he remains worth attending to.

Further Reading

The standard late nineteenth century Longman's edition of all Newman's published writings is available, free, online at <www.newmanreader.org/>. Except where an alternative edition of works by Newman is specifically indicated in the notes, citations are taken from this edition.

Three-large-scale biographies are standard points of reference. The first 'authorized' biography was by Wilfred Ward, son of W. G. Ward, once Newman's tractarian disciple, eventually one of his most determined Catholic opponents. Ward knew Newman personally, and was the most intelligent and sympathetic contemporary interpreter of his work. Published in 1912 at the height of the Modernist crisis, Ward's 1000 page book disposes of the Anglican career in 52 pages, plays down the more radical implications of Newman's thought, and emphasizes his submission to authority: but it is a classic of English 'life-writing' and retains its value.

Among modern biographies, two stand out: Ian Ker's *John Henry Newman*, (Oxford, 1990) is exhaustively based on the *Letters and Diaries* and Newman's published writings and provides almost day-by-day coverage. Sheridan Gilley's *Newman and His Age* (London, 1990) is a graceful account by a historian who is himself a convert to Catholicism from High-Church Anglicanism, with a strong literary sensibility.

Of the crop of shorter biographies elicited by Newman's

beatification, easily the best is John Cornwell's consciously provocative *Newman's Unquiet Grave* (London, 2010). David Newsome's *The Convert Cardinals* (London, 1993) is a masterly and on the whole balanced double-biography of Newman and his *bete noire,* Manning. Frank Turner's *John Henry Newman: the challenge to Evangelical Religion* (New Haven and London, 2002) was a ground-breaking study of the importance of Newman's rejection of Evangelicalism as a key to his Anglican years, but Turner's manifest loathing for the younger Newman distorts his reading of evidence and makes his book the case for the prosecution rather than a biography. Owen Chadwick's small volume in the Past Masters series, *Newman* (Oxford, 1983), is full of insight. The best short introduction to Newman's theology remains Stephen Dessain's *John Henry Newman* (London, 1966): a more recent survey, arranged by theme, is Avery Dulles, *Newman* (London, 2003).

There are many anthologies of Newman's writings: among the best are Vincent Fehrer Blehl (editor), *The Essential Newman* (New York, 1963) and Ian Ker (editor), *The Genius of John Henry Newman: selections from his writing* (Oxford, 2012).

Newman was the most prolific and arguably the best letter-writer of Victorian England: his collected *Letters and Diaries* have been published by Oxford University Press in thirty-two volumes (1961–2010) under the general editorship of Fr Stephen Dessain. The fullest single-volume selection is by Roderick Strange, *John Henry Newman, a portrait in letters* (Oxford, 2015), with valuable introductions providing a biographical overview. The delightful shorter selection by Joyce Sugg, *A Packet of Letters: Selections from the correspondence of John Henry Newman* (Oxford, 1993), remains valuable.

Further Reading

There is a Newman industry generating acres of monographs and essays, of very variable quality, on all aspects of his work. The most comprehensive recent collection, with useful essays on most of the topics covered in this book, is Frederick Aquino and Benjamin King (editors), *The Oxford Handbook of John Henry Newman* (Oxford, 2018). The best of many older collections is Ian Ker and Alan G. I. Hill (editors), *Newman after a Hundred Years* (Oxford, 1990): John Coulson and A. M. Allchin, (editors), *The Rediscovery of Newman: an Oxford Symposium* (London, 1967), was a pioneering ecumenical venture.

Chapter 1

For the general 19th century background, Owen Chadwick, *The Victorian Church* (2 vols, London, 1966, 1970): on Tractarianism, Peter Nockles, *The Oxford Movement in Context: Anglican High Churchmanship 1760–1857* (Cambridge, 1994), displaced all earlier interpretations. But R. W. Church's *The Oxford Movement: Twelve Years 1833–1845* (London 1891) remains a classic account by a participant: it is best read in the edition with an introduction by Geoffrey Best (Oxford, 1970). For the impact of Tractarianism in the parishes, G. Herring, *The Oxford Movement in Practice* (Oxford, 2016). On the Catholic Church Newman joined, Edward Norman, *The English Catholic Church in the Nineteenth Century* (Oxford, 1984) and Mary Heimann, *Catholic Devotion in Victorian England* (Oxford, 1995).

Chapter 2

On Newman's engagement with the Fathers of the early church: Benjamin King, *Newman and the Alexandrian Fathers* (Oxford, 2009): Stephen Thomas, *Newman and Heresy, the Anglican Years* (Cambridge, 1991): Roderick Strange, *Newman and the Gospel of Christ* (Oxford, 1981), and Rowan Williams' groundbreaking essay 'Newman's Arians and the Question of Method in Doctrinal History' in Ker and Hill, *Newman after a Hundred Years*.

On the Development of Doctrine, Owen Chadwick, *From Bossuet to Newman* (Cambridge, 1987): Nicholas Lash, *Newman on Development: the Search for an Explanation in History* (Sheperdstown, WV, 1975): Aidan Nicholas, *From Newman to Congar: the Idea of Doctrinal Development from the Victorians to the Second Vatican Council* (Edinburgh, 1990).

Chapter 3

The literature on Newman's philosophical work is mostly technical. But Thomas Vargish's study, *Newman: the Contemplation of Mind* (Oxford, 1970) is approachable, as are the essays by Basil Mitchell on 'Newman as a Philosopher' in Ker and Hill, *Newman after a Hundred Years*, Anthony Kenny's 'Newman as a Philosopher of Religion', in David Brown (editor), *Newman, A Man for Our Time* (London, 1990): and Gerard Hughes, 'Conscience' in Ian Ker and Terence Merrigan, *The Cambridge Companion to John Henry Newman* (Cambridge, 2009).

Chapter 11 'The Logic of the heart', and Chapter 12 'Newman and Empiricism' of J. M. Cameron's *The Night Battle* (London, 1962), are full of insight. Among older studies, A. J. Boekraad, *The Personal Conquest of Truth According to J. H. Newman* (Louvain, 1955), retains its value, but is scarce and hard to get hold of.

Chapter 4

For two accessible general introductions to Newman's thought, somewhat contrasting in emphasis, Avery Dulles,

John Henry Newman (London 2002), and Roderick Strange, *John Henry Newman, a Mind Alive* (London 2008). For the Infallibility crisis, in addition to the coverage in the biographies by Ward, Ker and Gilley, John R. Page's *What will Dr Newman Do? John Henry Newman and Papal Infallibility 1865–75* (Collegeville, 1994). For Newman's ecclesiology, the editor's introduction in John Coulson (editor), *On Consulting the Faithful in Matters of Doctrine* (Lanham, 1961): and John Coulson, *Newman and the Common Tradition* (Oxford, 1970). More cautious and qualified treatment in the essays by Avery Dulles and Francis Sullivan in Ker and Hill, *Newman after a Hundred Years*. For a fine study of the theology of Newman's opposite, Cardinal Manning, James Pereiro, *Cardinal Manning, from Anglican Archdeacon to Council Father at Vatican 1* (Leominster, 2008).

Chapter 5

There is no single satisfactory book on Newman as a literary figure. The first seven essays in Ker and Hill, N*ewman after a Hundred Years*, consider various aspects of his writing. On the sermons, see the essays in that collection by Eric Griffiths, and by Eamon Duffy in Aquino and King, *Handbook*: there is a good selection of the sermons by Ian Ker, *John Henry Newman, Selected Sermons* (New York, 1994). All the *Parochial and Plain Sermons* have been republished in a handsome and handy single volume by Ignatius Press (San Francisco, 1997). The best study of Newman's educational ideals, and of *The Idea of a University*, remains A. Dwight Culler, *The Imperial Intellect* (New Haven and London, 1955): Colin Barr's *Paul Cullen, John Henry Newman and the Catholic University of Ireland 1845–1865* (Leominster, 2003) replaces all previous studies of the historical context. David de Laura, *Hebrew and Hellene in Victorian England: Newman, Arnold and Pater* (University of Texas, 1969) is an illuminating comparative study. The standard scholarly edition of the *Apologia* is edited by Martin Svaglic (Oxford, 1967). There is a convenient paperback from Penguin (Harmondsworth, 1994) edited by Ian Ker. Some background is provided in Linda Peterson, *Victorian Autobiography* (London, 1986).

Chapter 6

For the reception of Newman's thought and his continuing legacy, see the section 'Ongoing Significance' in Aquino and King, *Handbook* (pp. 495–596) and Aquino and King (editors), *Receptions of Newman* (Oxford, 2015). Important older treatments in the essays by B. D. Dupuy, Werner Becker, H. Francis Davis, and B. C. Butler in Coulson and Allchin, *The Rediscovery of Newman*, pp. 147–226, and the essay by Nicholas Lash in Ker and Hill, *Newman After a Hundred Years*, pp. 447–464. On the complicated issue of Newman's work on the doctrine of Justification, in addition to the relevant sections of the surveys by Dulles and Strange, Henry Chadwick, 'The Lectures on Justification', in I. Ker and A. Hill, (eds), *Newman After a Hundred Years*: Alister McGrath, 'Newman on Justification, an Anglican Evangelical Evaluation', in T. Merrigan and I. Ker (eds), *Newman and the Word* (Leuven, 2000), pp. 91–107: David Newsome, 'Justification and Sanctification: Newman and the Evangelicals', *Journal of Theological Studies*, vol. 15 (1964), pp. 32–53 and the same author's 'The Evangelical sources of Newman's power', in John Coulson and D. Allchin (eds), *The Rediscovery of Newman*: Thomas L. Sheridan, 'Newman and Luther on Justification', *Journal of Ecumenical Studies*, vol.

38 (2001), pp. 217–45: for a more hostile critique, Joseph S. O'Leary, 'Impeded Witness: Newman against Luther on Justification', in David Nicholls and Fergus Kerr, *John Henry Newman, Reason, Rhetoric and Romanticism* (Bristol, 1991), pp. 153–93.

Notes

1 J. D Walsh, 'Joseph Milner's Evangelical Church History', *Journal of Ecclesiastical History*, Vol.10 (1959), pp.174–87.
2 C. S. Dessain et al (eds), *The Letters and Diaries of John Henry Newman* (31 volumes plus supplementary volume 32, 1961–2008) (hereafter *Letters & Diaries*); *Letters & Diaries*, vol. 25, p. 231 to Lady Simeon Nov. 18 1870.
3 *Letters & Diaries* vol. 25, p. 430, to Malcolm McColl, Nov. 11 1871.
4 *Parochial and Plain Sermons*, vol 1 pp. 320–1.
5 Owen Chadwick, *Newman* (Oxford, 1983), pp. 17–26.
6 *Discussions and Arguments*, p. 268.
7 *Letters & Diaries*, vol. 5, pp. 301–4, to Hugh James Rose, May 23 1836.
8 *Apologia Pro Vita Sua*, edited by Martin Svaglic (Oxford, 1967), pp. 155–6.
9 Rowan Williams, 'Newman's Arians', in Ian Ker and Alan Hill (eds), *Newman After a Hundred Years* (Oxford, 1990), pp. 263–85.
10 *An Essay on the Development of Christian Doctrine* (London, 1903), Ch. 1, section 1, p. 40.
11 *Autobiographical Writings*, edited by H. Tristram (New York, 1957), p. 255.
12 The nadir of his depression over all this is harrowingly recorded in *Autobiographical Writings*, pp. 249–60.
13 *Apologia*, p. 217.
14 Edmund Sheridan Purcell, *Life of Cardinal Manning*, vol. 2 (London, 1896), p. 323.

15 *Letters & Diaries*, vol. 25, pp. 18-19, to Bishop Ullathorne, Jan. 28 1870.
16 *Grammar of Assent*, Ian Ker (ed) (Oxford, 1985), pp. 66–7.
17 Anthony Kenny, 'Newman as a philosopher of religion', in David Brown (ed), *Newman, a Man for Our Time* (London, 1990), pp. 98–122.
18 *Letters & Diaries*, vol. 29, p. 72, to Richard Church, Mar. 11 1879.
19 *Apologia*, p. 36.
20 John Henry Newman, *Selected Writings to 1845*, Albert Radcliffe (ed) (Manchester, 2002), . 104.
21 *Lectures on the Prophetical Office of the Church viewed relative to Romanism and Popular Protestantism* (London, 1837), pp. 62–3.
22 *Arians of the Fourth Century*, with an introduction and notes by Rowan Williams (Leominster, 2001), p. xxxvi.
23 *Arians*, pp 30–1, 106: the targeting of theological liberalism in *Arians* is illuminatingly explored in Stephen Thomas, *Newman and Heresy, the Anglican Years* (Cambridge, 1991), pp. 36–49.
24 *Apologia*, pp. 36–7.
25 *Arians*, p. 180.
26 *Arians*, pp. 36–7.
27 *Letters & Diaries*, vol. 25, pp. 18–19, to Bishop Ullathorne, Jan. 28 1870.
28 *Lectures on Justification*, p. 218–9.
29 *Parochial and Plain Sermons*, vol 6, p 62
30 *The Catechetical Lectures of St Cyril, Archbishop of Jerusalem, in The Library of the Fathers* (1839), p. xviii.
31 *Letters & Diaries*, vol. 6, p. 6, to his sister Jemima, Jan. 5 1837.
32 *Prophetical Office*, pp. 297–300, 308.
33 See below, p. 67–72.
34 *Apologia*, p. 108.
35 Ker, *John Henry Newman*, p. 177–8.
36 *Apologia*, pp. 110–1.
37 The essay was reprinted in *Essays Critical and Historical*, vol. 2, pp. 1–73.

38 They are a staple of the 'Samaritan' sermons published in *Sermons on Subjects of the Day* in 1843.
39 Ker, *Newman*, p. 184.
40 *An Essay on the Development of Christian Doctrine*, pp. 7–8.
41 *Letters & Diaries*, vol. 7, pp 436–44, to Francis Newman, Nov. 10 1840.
42 *Fifteen Sermons preached before the University of Oxford*, David Earnest Janes and Gerard Tracey (eds) (Oxford, 2006), p. 218.
43 *Development*, p. 29.
44 *Development*, p. 38.
45 *Development*, p. 56.
46 I have used the later form of the seven 'tests' or 'notes', as set out in *Development*, pp. 171 ff.
47 Appendix 3 to the edition of the *Essay* edited by James Tollhurst (Gracewing: Leominster, 2018) helpfully documents the changes Newman made for the standard 1878 edition.
48 *Letters & Diaries*, vol. 20, p. 224, to Sir John Acton, July 8 1862.
49 *Development*, pp. 272–3.
50 *Letters & Diaries*, vol. 25, p. 280, to H. J. Coleridge, Feb. 3 1871.
51 *Letters & Diaries*, vol. 20, p. 224, to Sir John Acton, Jul. 8 1862.
52 *The Works of the Most Reverend Dr John Tillotson* (London, 1722), vol. 1 p. 18.
53 Richard Whately, *Easy Lessons in Christian Evidences* (London, 1838), p. 18.
54 William Paley's *Natural Theology: Evidences of the being and Attributes of the Deity*, collected from the *Appearances of Nature* (London, 1802).
55 Coleridge, *Aids to Reflection* (Bohn's Library edition, London, 1913), p. 272.
56 *Fifteen Sermons*, p. 138.
57 Tamworth Reading Room in *Discussions and Arguments*, p. 293.
58 *Fifteen Sermons*, pp. 177–8.
59 *Fifteen Sermons*, p. 178.
60 *Fifteen Sermons*, p. 137.

61 *Fifteen Sermons*, p. 151.
62 *Sermons preached on Various Occasions*, pp. 64–5.
63 *The Grammar of Assent*, Ian Ker (ed) (Oxford, 1985), p. 76.
64 *Grammar of Assent*, p. 224.
65 *Grammar of Assent*, pp. 231–2.
66 *Letters & Diaries*, vol. 21, p. 146, to Canon J. Walker of Scarborough, Jul. 6 1864: for a recent discussion of Butler's influence on Newman, Jane Garnett, 'Joseph Butler' in Frederick Aquino and Benjamin King (eds), *Oxford Handbook of John Henry Newman* (Oxford, 2019), pp. 135–153.
67 *Letters & Diaries*, vol. 29, p. 114, to William Froude, April 29 1879. Froude never read the letter, as he died in South Africa before its arrival.
68 For parallels between Newman and Wittgenstein, Angelo Bottone, 'Newman and Wittgenstein after Foundationalism', *New Blackfriars*, vol. 86, no. 1001 (January, 2005), pp. 62–75.
69 The quoted phrase is from the memorandum on the Catholic University in *Autobiographical Writings*, H. Tristram (ed) (New York, 1957), p. 320: cf. 'If ever there was a power on earth who had an eye for the times, who has confined himself to the practicable… whose words have been facts, and whose commands prophecies, such is he in the history of ages, who sits from generation to generation in the Chair of the Apostles, as the Vicar of Christ, and the Doctor of His Church.' *Idea of a University*, p. 13.
70 *Letters & Diaries*, vol. 14, pp. 365–6, to Francis Richard Wegg-Prosser, Sept. 24 1851.
71 John Coulson (ed), *On Consulting the Faithful in Matters of Doctrine* (London, 1961), pp. 63, 76.
72 E. Duffy, *Saints and Sinners, a History of the Popes*, 3rd Ed. (Yale University Press, CT: 2006), p. 291.
73 Newman, *Certain Difficulties felt by Anglicans in Catholic Teaching Considered*, vol. 1, pp. 178–9.
74 *The Rambler,* New Series, vol. 1 (May 1859), p. 102.

75 *Letters & Diaries*, vol. 19, p. 449–50, to Miss Holmes, Jan. 10 1861.
76 *The Pope and the Revolution: a sermon preached in the Oratory Church, Birmingham, on Sunday, October 7th 1866* (London, 1866).
77 *Letters & Diaries*, vol. 22, pp. 302–3, to T. W. Allies, Oct. 21 1866.
78 *Letters & Diaries*, vol. 23, pp. 142–3, to James Hope Scott,Apr. 11 1867.
79 *Letters & Diaries*, vol. 22, pp. 314–5, to Emily Bowles, Nov. 11 1866.
80 *Letters & Diaries*, vol. 2,4 pp. 212–3 to Maria Giberne, Feb. 10 1869 and see also vol. 20, p. 353, to William Monsell, Nov. 14 1862.
81 C. S. Dessain, *John Henry Newman*, 2nd Ed. (Stanford, 1971), p. 124.
82 *Letters & Diaries*, vol. 11, p. 293, to W. G. Penny, Dec. 13 1846 (on Fr Peronne's limitations as a theologian).
83 *Letter to the Duke of Norfolk in Difficulties of Anglicans*, vol. 2, section 7, pp. 294–5.
84 *Letters & Diaries*, vol. 11, p. 196, to J. D. Dalgairns, Jul. 6 1846: Wilfred Ward, *Life of Cardinal Newman*, vol. 1, p. 123 ff.
85 *Letters & Diaries*, vol. 22, pp. 215–6, to Emily Bowles, Apr. 16 1866.
86 *Letters & Diaries*, vol. 27, pp. 212–3 to Lord Blatchford, Feb. 5 1875.
87 *Apologia*, p. 226.
88 *Letters & Diaries*, vol. 26, pp. 59-60, to J. Spencer Northcote, Apr. 7 1872.
89 *Letters & Diaries*, vol. 20, pp. 445–8, to Emily Bowles, May 19 1863.
90 *Letters & Diaries*, vol. 21, p. 386, to William Monsell, Jan. 12 1865.
91 E. B. Pusey, *The Church of England a portion of Christ's one true Catholic Church… an Eirenicon* (London and Oxford, 1865).

92 Letter to Pusey in *Difficulties of Anglicans*, vol. 2, pp. 20–1.
93 Letter to Pusey, pp. 23-4.
94 Edmund Sheridan Purcell, *Life of Cardinal Manning* (London 1896), vol. 2, p. 323.
95 *Letters & Diaries*, vol. 24, p. 323, note 2.
96 Ker, *Newman*, p. 635.
97 *Letters & Diaries*, vol. 25, pp. 18–20, to Bishop Ullathorne, Jan. 28 1870.
98 *Letters & Diaries*, vol. 25, p. 231, to Lady Simeon, Nov. 18 1870.
99 *Letters & Diaries*, vol. 25, pp. 308–10, to Alfred Plummer, Apr. 3 1871.
100 *Letters & Diaries*, vol. 22, p. 317, to Bishop David Moriarty, Nov.14 1866
101 *Letters & Diaries*, vol. 25, p. 262, to Mrs William Froude, Jan. 2 1871.
102 Alvin Ryan (ed), *Newman and Gladstone, the Vatican Decrees* (Notre Dame, IN, 1962), pp/ 167–70.
103 *Newman and Gladstone*, p. 138.
104 *Newman and Gladstone*, pp. 129, 133.
105 *Newman and Gladstone*, p. 151.
106 *Newman and Gladstone*, pp. 153, 166.
107 *Newman and Gladstone*, p. 166.
108 *Letters & Diaries*, vol. 20, pp. 445–8, to Emily Bowles, May 19 1863.
109 *Letters & Diaries*, vol. 20, p. 426, to Robert Ormsby, Mar. 26 1863.
110 *Letters & Diaries*, vol. 27, p. 70, to Lord Blachford, June 3 1874.
111 Nicholas Lash, *Theology on Dover Beach* (London, 1979), p. 103.
112 J. H. Newman, *The Via Media of the Anglican Church Illustrated in Lectures, Letters and Tracts written between 1830 and 1841.... with a Preface and Notes* (London, 1877), vol. 1, p. xli.
113 *Via Media*, p. xlii.
114 *Via Media*, pp. xlvii–xlviii.
115 John Coulson, *Newman and the Common Tradition* (Oxford 1970), pp. 165–78.

116 *Via Media*, p. xciv.

117 For the First Vatican Council's decree on revelation, including the section on the inspiration of scripture which worried Newman, Norman P. Tanner (ed), *Decrees of the Ecumenical Councils* (Georgetown University Press, 1990), vol. 2, p 806.

118 What follows is based on the analysis of Newman's views in the introduction to *On the Inspiration of Scripture*, edited by J. Derek Holmes and Robert Murray (Washington, 1967), pp 3–98: Newman's earlier manuscript writings on Scripture were edited by J. Derek Holmes in *The Theological Papers of John Henry Newman on Biblical Inspiration and on Infallibility* (Oxford, 1979).

119 Rowland E. Prothero, *Life and Letters of Dean Stanley* (London, 1 volume edition, 1909), pp. 445–8.

120 *Letters & Diaries*, vol. 13, p. 419, to Miss G Munro, Feb. 11 1850.

121 *Callista*, pp. 314–5.

122 *The Dream of Gerontius and other Poems by John Henry Newman* (Oxford, 1914), p. 3.

123 For 'penitence and community' in Dante's *Purgatorio*, Robin Kirkpatrick (editor and translator), Dante, *Purgatorio* (Harmondsworth, 2007), pp. xxvi–xxxviii: the Newman phrase is from *Apologia*, p .18.

124 Seamus Deane (ed), *Portrait of the Artist as a Young Man* (Penguin, 2000), pp. 179, 190. The line Dedalus quoted is from Newman's panagyric on the papacy in the first of his University Discourses in *Idea of a University*, p. 14.

125 *Letters & Diaries*, vol. 24, p. 241, to John Hayes, Apr 13 1869.

126 David de Laura, 'O Unforgotten Voice: the Memory of Newman in the Nineteenth century', in *Sources for Interpretation: the Use of Nineteenth century Literary Documents: Essays in honor of C L Cline* (University of Texas at Austin, TX: 1975), pp. 23–55.

127 *Parochial and Plain Sermons*, vol. 5, p. 44.

128 *Parochial and Plain Sermons*, vol. 1, p. 13, 'Promising without doing', 173.
129 *Sermons on Subjects of the Day*, p. 307.
130 Michael de la Bedoyere, *The Life of Baron Von Hugel* (London, 1951), pp. 31–2.
131 *Idea of a University*, p. 14.
132 *Idea of a University*, pp. 120–1.
133 *Idea of a University*, pp. 208–11.
134 *Idea of a University*, pp. 229–30.
135 *Idea of a University*, p. 476.
136 *Idea of a University*, pp. 466–7.
137 H. Tristram (ed), *Autobiographical Writings* (New York, 1957), p. 5.
138 Owen Chadwick, 'Bremond and Newman', in *The Spirit of the Oxford Movement: Tractarian Essays* (Cambridge, 1990), p. 181.
139 *Letters & Diaries*, vol. 20, p. 443, to his sister Jemima, May 18 1863: *Historical Sketches*, vol. 2, p. 221: he was discussing the letters of the Fathers, especially St John Chrysostom.
140 *Letters & Diaries*, vol. 24, pp. 362–3, to Archbishop Manning, Nov. 3 1869: *Letters & Diaries*, vol. 23, pp. 216–7, to W. G. Ward, May 9 1867.
141 *Letters & Diaries*, vol. 29, p. 241, to his nephew, John Rickards Mozley, Feb 26 1880.
142 *Apologia*, p. 15.
143 *Autobiographical Writings*, p. 254.
144 *Apologia*, pp. 385-464.
145 *Apologia*, p. 406.
146 *Discussions and Arguments*, p. 294.
147 *Fifteen Sermons*, pp. 176-7.
148 *Apologia*, p. 137.
149 *Apologia*, p. 155–6.
150 *Letters & Diaries*, vol. 20, pp. 215–6, to the editor of the Globe, June 28 1862.
151 *Apologia*, p. 213.

152 Blehl & Connolly, *Newman's Apologia*, p. 59.
153 F. W. Newman, *Contributions chiefly to the Early History of Cardinal Newman* (London, 1891), p. 117.
154 Edwin A. Abbott, *The Anglican Career of Cardinal Newman* (London, 1892).
155 F. L. Cross, *Newman* (Glasgow, 1933), pp. 54-5.
156 R. W. Church, *The Oxford Movement* (London, 1891).
157 *Apologia*, p. 76.
158 Simon Skinner, 'Newman, the Tractarians, and the British Critic', *Journal of Ecclesiastical History*, vol. 50, no. 4 (October 1999), pp. 716–59.
159 Above, pp. 16, 26, 95–6.
160 *Apologia*, p. 238–9.
161 Above, p. 59.
162 Above, p. 61.
163 Von Hugel to Ward, 23 November 1911, cited in Laurence Barmann, *Baron Friederich von Hugel and the Modernist crisis in England* (Cambridge, 1972), p. 5 note 2.
164 G. Egner, *Apologia Pro Charles Kingsley* (London, 1969): see also Fitzpatrick's two essays in David Nicholls and Fergus Kerr (eds), *John Henry Newman: Reason, Rhetoric and Romanticism* (Bristol, 1991): the volume was a group attempt to deconstruct Newman's reputation.
165 Frank M. Turner, *John Henry Newman: the Challenge to Evangelical Religion* (New Haven, CT and London, 2002).
166 Simon Skinner, 'History Vs Hagiography: the Reception of Turner's Newman', *Journal of Ecclesiastical History*, vol. 61 (2010), p. 765.
167 Frank Turner (ed), *Apologia Pro Vita Sua and Six Sermons* (New Haven, CT and London, 2008), p. 85.
168 Turner, *Newman*, p .151.
169 Turner, *Apologia*, p. 104–5.
170 Turner, *Newman*, p. 533
171 Turner, *Newman*, p. 466.
172 Turner, *Newman*, pp. 139–42.

173 For example, Tristram Hunt in the *Guardian,* Saturday January 4 2003.

174 See Tatchell's article on the exhumation, in the *Guardian,* September 4 2008.

175 *Letters & Diaries*, vol. 6, p. 133, to Lord Lifford, Sept. 12 1837.

176 Turner, *Newman*, pp. 228–9.

177 Turner, *Newman*, p. 235.

178 *Difficulties of Anglicans*, p. 28.

179 *Apologia*, pp. 218–9.

180 Erik Sidenvall, *After Anti-Catholicism: John Henry Newman and Protestant Britain, 1845–c. 1890* (London, 2005), pp. 156–9.

181 Manning's Homily is printed in full in Edmund Purcell, *Life of Cardinal Manning*, vol. 2 (London, 1896), pp. 749–52.

182 *Letters & Diaries*, vol. 25, p. 58, to Bishop David Moriarty, Mar. 20 1871.

183 R. F. Clarke S. J., *Logic* (Stonyhurst, 1909), cited in Nicholas Sagovsky, 'Frustration, disillusion and enduring filial respect: George Tyrell's debt to John Henry Newman', in Mary Jo Weaver (ed), *Newman and the Modernists* (Lanham and London, 1985), p. 99.

184 Gabriel Daly, *Transcendence and Immanence: a Study in Catholic Modernism and Integralism* (Oxford, 1980), pp. 7–25: Nicholas Lash, 'Newman and A Firmin', in A. H. Jenkins (ed), *John Henry Newman and Modernism* (Sigmaringendorf, 1990), p. 59.

185 Aidan Nichol, *From Newman to Congar* (Edinburgh, 1990), pp. 129–35.

186 The Pastoral Letter is printed in Weaver, *Newman and the Modernists*, pp. 131–57.

187 Weaver, *Newman and the Modernists*, pp. 83, 85, 109.

188 Mark McInroy, 'Theological Receptions of the *Grammar*, in Frederick D. Aquino and Benjamin J. King (eds), *Receptions of Newman* (Oxford, 2015), pp. 77–85. And see the essay by B. D. Dupuy, 'Newman's influence in France', in John Coulson

and A. M. Allchin (eds), *The Rediscovery of Newman* (London, 1967), especially pp. 147–69.

189 Cited by Werner Becker in Coulson and Allchin, *Rediscovery of Newman*, p. 180.

190 See the essay by Mark McInroy, 'Catholic Theological Reception', in Aquino and King, *Handbook*, pp. 506–7.

191 Joseph Ratzinger, Speech at the commemoration of the centenary of the death of Newman, Rome April 28 1990: available on the Vatican website, <http://www.vatican.va/roman_curia/congregations/cfaith/documents/rc_con_cfaith_doc_19900428_ratzinger-newman_en.html>.

192 Essay by Geoffrey Rowell in Aquino and King, *Handbook*, p. 525.

193 Hans Kung, *Justification* (London, 1963), p. 203.

194 *Lectures on Justification*, p. 340.

195 McInroy, in *Handbook*, p. 512.

196 Ratzinger, Speech at the commemoration of the centenary of the death of Newman, Rome, April 28 1990.

197 J. Derek Holmes (ed), *The Theological Papers of John Henry Newman on Biblical Inspiration and on Infallibility* (Oxford, 1979), p 97.

198 Both quoted in Nicholas Lash, 'Newman since Vatican II', in Ker and Hill, *Newman After a Hundred Years*, p. 459.

199 Owen Chadwick, *Acton and History* (Cambridge, 1998), p. 132.

Index